Lives in Cricket: No 9

J.H.King
Leicestershire's Longaevous Left-Hander

A.R.Littlewood

With a foreword by Philip Snow

First published in Great Britain by
Association of Cricket Statisticians and Historians
Cardiff CF11 9XR
© ACS, 2009

A.R.Littlewood has asserted his right under the Copyright, Designs and Patents Act 1988 to be identified as the author of this work.

All Rights Reserved. No part of this publication may be reproduced, stored in a retrieval system, or transmitted in any form, or by any means, electronic, mechanical, photocopying, recording or otherwise without the prior permission in writing of the Copyright holders, nor be otherwise circulated in any form, or binding or cover other than in which it is published and without a similar condition including this condition being imposed on the subsequent publisher.

British Library Cataloguing-in-Publication Data.
A catalogue record for this book is available from the British Library.

ISBN: 978 1 905138 71 5
Typeset by Limlow Books

To my wife,
who though not born to it has learned to love
the game.

John Herbert King in his England cap.

Contents

Foreword		6
Preface		10
Chapter One:	Early Days	11
Chapter Two:	Apprenticeship	18
Chapter Three:	Technique and Style	28
Chapter Four:	From Journeyman to Master	45
Chapter Five:	The Match of the Season	55
Chapter Six:	Successes and Disappointments	60
Chapter Seven:	The Test-Match Player	69
Chapter Eight:	Maturity	76
Chapter Nine:	Interlude	91
Chapter Ten:	Nestor	95
Chapter Eleven:	Retirement	112
Chapter Twelve:	Albert Knight's Appreciation	119
Chapter Thirteen:	His Place in Leicestershire's Annals	123
Acknowledgements		129
Bibliography		131
Appendix One:	Some Statistics	134
Appendix Two:	King's Only Test Match	140
Index		143

Foreword
by Philip Snow, OBE

It is timely that, in the present era dominated vulgarly by the money-getting mania encapsulated in simplistic and stultifying slog-and-scamper spectacles, utterly valueless in history, this erudite and knowledgeable work has appeared. Illustrating graphically the elegant technique of an accomplished exponent, both before the 1914-18 War and for seven years after, this study with its fine research adds to both knowledge and nostalgia. Without, I hope, discounting too much its pleasing flavour, I can only add a few tangential reminiscences.

At the age of six I was taken by my elder brothers, Harold, Charles and Eric - through whom I was to meet J.H.King's daughter, Margaret Wearn, and grand-daughter, Judy Cockroft, both of them with the family's striking looks - to see in 1921 Leicestershire versus the strongest-ever Australians, matched by Bradman's 1948 team. I still have vivid memories of the day, probably because of the animated discussion there was around the crowded popular stand on the Aylestone Road ground about the differing and deadly styles of J.M.Gregory, with his leaps and bounds and slings, so well caricatured in *The Cricketer* as a demented kangaroo, and E.A.McDonald, with greater speed and the most graceful, smoothest of actions like Larwood's. I cannot recall any other player seen, although one would have been King. The queue to enter the ground had seemed interminable, as did the series of clanking, special trams to disgorge impatient spectators-to-be before branching off to line up for the day a dozen deep alongside a Cattle Market pasture. Yes, I would have seen King on the field - perhaps no longer in his prime - but I saw him without seeing him. The reason? I was still dazzled by Gregory and McDonald. King, going in at No.3, was second out with 29, the second highest score of the innings. That was at the very beginning of the three-day match, which lasted only two days, and I had been there with the crowd, pushing in from the start. King did not bowl and was absent hurt for the second innings.

Foreword

I began to watch Leicestershire regularly from 1927 and would come to recognize the imposing figure of King from pictures in the County Ground pavilion and on his occasional visits in retirement when we were both on top of trams taking us to our respective destinations in Aylestone Park not too far apart. It might be said that he carried a benign, stately presence wherever he was.

I came to know well his elder brother, James, who also played for the county. As licensee of the Avenue Hotel on Cavendish Road, Aylestone Park, adjoining Richmond Road, where our family house was, he had a rather broken-down wooden garage at the back. He agreed that I could park my equally broken-down Morris Cowley in it, as it was illegal to park on roads without lights overnight, although streets were mostly empty, and car batteries were not easily come by. James was perhaps a cut above the typical pub licensee. For a breath of fresh air at the end of closing time he would declare in a cultured tone that he would take a stroll, and then he would walk to Cavendish Road via Lansdowne Road, passing our house on the way back to his pub, followed by two dogs without leads and a very large tabby cat matching his majestic pace. I thought him solemn, like his son J.W., whose lack of success with Worcestershire and Leicestershire was a deep disappointment.

On 21 August 1940 James' hotel had a very near miss when, in daylight, a German aeroplane dropped a string of bombs, Leicester's first ever, along the terraced houses on the opposite side of Cavendish Road, killing nine, including some of his customers, and shattering the rear windows of our house.

J.H.King I came to know as Jack from his brother's references about him to me. When I eventually met him, I of course never addressed him as other than Mr King.

In the spring of 1934 I was anxious to obtain any sort of practice for my last year in the Alderman Newton's School team, where my opening partner was Maurice Tompkin. (He toured Pakistan with an MCC team and there has been no more distinguished Newtonian cricketer before or since.) I cajoled a junior friend from the nearby Saffron Lane estate – he was to be the father of Rosie Winterton, now Minister of State at the Department for Work and Pensions – to bowl to me. He was as wildly lacking in direction as Harmison. We were on a sports ground, the whole turf covered with plantains from the canal alongside flooding in winters, when

7

a figure familiar to me came from the towpath asking if he could join us. I was only too glad to banish my friend to retrieving shots from J.H.King and myself. Taking off his blue serge jacket, King bowled with as high an action as I was ever to see. At a slow pace he made the ball jump, skid and fall on the plantains to rap my padless legs amid his apologies. In his turn he stroked the ball to the off and away from his legs with ease. After about an hour we accompanied King across the canal to leave him at his house in Aylestone Road near its junction with Duncan Road, which leads to the Grace Road ground. The house is still there, and Sylvia Michael, the outstanding county Honorary Archivist living on Park Hill Avenue,[1] remembers crossing Aylestone Road as a child to fetch sweets being sold there in the War. When Winterton and I left King at his gate, there was a complaint about feeling weary, which I silenced with: 'It isn't every day that you field to an England player.' Looking back now, that was a shade dismissive, I feel, and I hope that I did not put him off cricket for life.

In my final year at Christ's College, Cambridge, I noticed that King was to umpire a match at Fenner's, and I wrote to invite him to lunch with me in Hall. In my four years there I never saw anyone other than of undergraduate age and from other colleges eat there (apart from on High Table), but I had few misgivings when he accepted, as his demeanour was always inflexibly gentlemanly. Meeting him at the College gate, I took him to the rooms of my brother, C.P.Snow, who was a Fellow and Tutor and would eat at High Table. King was delighted when Charles told him that he had often seen him in his playing days on the Aylestone Road ground, recalling in particular when he was sixteen the devastation of McDonald and Gregory there. Who could forget it? I was not sure how undergraduate conversation would flow in Hall with someone so much older. I had invited Norman Yardley, captain of the University, successful with Yorkshire and noted by my brother in his regular column in the late 1930s in *The Cricketer* under the pseudonym 'XX' as potentially a captain of England, to join us from his college. As President of the Hawks' Club for a select few Blues, near or Half Blues in all games, Yardley had piloted my election to it. I was captain of the Christ's team and saw to it that half of the side sat near King, who told me how pleased he was to have just learned from Yardley that I had been captain of the Leicestershire Second Eleven for three years in the long vacations.

---

1   Sadly Sylvia Michael died shortly before this book went to press.

As I was due to take up an appointment as Administrator in the South Pacific, there was no further opportunity to see a memorable, courteous, professional personality, full of wisdom, patience and breeding, of whom I was always hearing in talks with George Geary, Ewart Astill (his biography calls out to be written), Alan Shipman, Aubrey Sharp, Tommy Sidwell, Gordon Salmon and Frank Bale when I came to know these contemporaries of his. Of King's talent and achievement we are pointedly reminded in this comprehensive survey by Antony Littlewood, Professor of Classics at the University of Western Ontario, whose grammar school was that also of Albert Knight, with his liking for Classics, who played for England in Australia and wrote so discerningly of his friend, Jack King. One is of course left wondering, as with many of King's contemporaries, what further feats King would have accomplished, although virtually past his prime of life – though able to score 205 in 1923 when fifty-two years old – had he not been engulfed by the 1914-18 War.

Editor's Note: Philip Snow played cricket regularly for Leicestershire's Second Eleven in the thirties, captaining the side in 1936, 1937 and 1938. He was a member of the Colonial Administrative Service in the Pacific from 1937 to 1952, and was captain of the Fijian side which toured New Zealand in 1947/48, playing seventeen matches, five of which were retrospectively ruled first-class by the International Cricket Conference in 1988. He was the Fijian representative on the ICC from 1964 to 1994: in 1970 he was made an Honorary Life Member of MCC for his services to international cricket. His older brother, Charles, was a celebrated novelist, who became Lord Snow of Leicester in 1964 and a minister in the Wilson government of 1964 to 1966. Another brother, Eric, was a member of the ACS for many years and wrote several books on Leicestershire cricket. The first of these, published in 1949, was a model for many later county histories.

Preface

It is always hard to write the biography of a cricketer who made his début over a hundred years ago and died over sixty years ago, whom nobody now alive saw in his prime and who rarely reached national consciousness and therefore much comment in the game's history books. But there were many worthy county players who were far more than just artisans, having in their time a devoted local following which they delighted with their skill and artistry in an age when county patriotism was still strong and county teams were viewed as valuable in their own right and not as mere nurseries for national blooms, and when there were no cries for the retirement of a highly successful and popular cricketer in his thirties to make room for a callow youngster who might just possibly one day play a few matches for England.

Sixteen years ago in a conversation with Mike Turner, Leicestershire's Chief Executive at the time, I expressed the opinion that an interesting book could be written on the county's all-rounders. Mike urged me to write such a book, overcoming my protests that I could not start until I had retired and that residence in the remoteness of Canada would fatally injure such a project; and on visits to England for other purposes I began to visit, through Mike's good offices, those who had played with or otherwise knew my chosen Leicestershire heroes. This short book on John Herbert King is now the first fruit of that conversation. Philip Snow made it possible by introducing me to King's daughter, Margaret Wearn, from whom in two long afternoon visits and numerous letters I learned much knowledge otherwise unattainable. I hope that I repaid her in part for her kindness and friendship by taking her up early one morning to Leicestershire to wander through our mutual rural childhood haunts before going to Grace Road, where we were royally entertained by Mike and watched Leicestershire play Yorkshire, so often opponents of her father and on one memorable occasion victims of his greatest bowling triumph.

No reader can be as aware as I of the inadequacies of the following narrative. I merely hope that I have rescued some scraps from the inexorable jaws of *tempus edax rerum*.

A.R.Littlewood
London, Ontario
January, 2009

Chapter One
Early Days

Unlike that of most of his contemporary professionals, the parentage of John Herbert King was comfortably middle-class; and seems to have been so for some generations. A mourning ring still in the family's possession, and containing some crocheted hair under glass surrounded by a circle of seed pearls, commemorates a Matilda King who was born on 7 July 1740 and died in 1805; she was in all probability King's great-great grandmother. He was also related, in some way which cannot now be accurately determined, to Colonel John King of Stretton, a fact of which his brother James was very proud, since he had asked Eric Snow to mention this fact 'casually' in his *History of Leicestershire Cricket* and then thanked him for promising to do exactly that.[2]

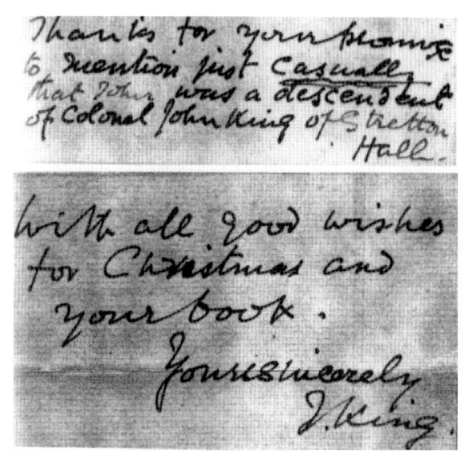

James King's letter thanking Eric Snow for agreeing to refer 'casually' to his claim to a landed ancestry.

---

2 This appears to be a reference to Lt-Col John King, who was a landowner at Stretton-under-Fosse (residing at Stretton Hall), about five miles from Lutterworth, in the nineteenth century. Colonel King held land also at Noseley, in the east of the county, in which area the Hazlerigg family – two of them were county captains – had long been prominent. James King may thus have perhaps been trying to point out that his own family history could be measured against that of the Hazleriggs.

Early Days

His father, James Temple King, was born around 1818 probably in Medbourne on the county boundary with Northamptonshire, and had been a day-boy at Uppingham School in neighbouring Rutland, riding there and back and stabling his pony during school hours at 'The Falcon'. Later he worked under the celebrated architect Sir Gilbert Scott and was himself responsible for building churches at Peterborough and Wisbech and restoring that at Rockingham. At some point he moved to Lutterworth, where he was for many years a prominent builder in the firm of Law, which in time became Law and King, and was entrusted with the most important project of his time in the district, the restoration of the roof of the parish church of Saint Mary, which involved the employment of 66 carpenters. The church was originally founded in the twelfth century on or near the site of the original Anglo-Saxon settlement Lutteres Vording (Luther's Farm) and still retains traces of thirteenth-century work and mediaeval frescos of crowned figures hawking and of Judgement Day; although it is best known to-day

Comfortably middle-class. King's father, James Temple King, attended Uppingham School and was a prominent figure in Lutterworth.

St Mary's Church, Lutterworth, in 2006. Restored by the family building business, it figured regularly in King's life.

for its late fourteenth-century rector, John Wycliffe, who from here under the protection of John of Gaunt attacked both the beliefs and practices of the Church and instigated the translation of the Bible into the vernacular. Fittingly the nineteenth-century builder became a much respected mason of the local Wiclif Lodge.

James Temple King begat two sons, William and Charles, by a first wife whose name is unknown, before he married Ann Cole of Lutterworth. Ann, born herself in 1829, was descended from a long-serving soldier described in Nichols' *History and Antiquities of Leicestershire*, based in part on the Visitation of Lutterworth (at that time merely a large agricultural village) on 21 March 1681, as 'William Cole Esq. of Lutterworth Ad. 67 in 1681. A Captain in the Services of King Charles Ist and in 1681 Major of the Trained Bands in Leicestershire and in commission of the Peace. . . . Buried at Laughton'. The memorial at Laughton vouchsafes further information: 'Here underneath on the North side of Barbra Cole [his first wife, daughter of the second son of Sir Richard Halford of Wistow] lyeth interred the Body of Col. William Cole Esq. who served His Majesty King Charles Ist. of Blessed Memory and three Kings his successors. 58 Years a Commission Officer Who departed this Life March 27th 1698 in the 85th Year of his age.' The 'three Kings' were Charles II, whose return he aided upon the collapse of the Commonwealth, James II and William III.

William Cole also became Lord of the Manor at Laughton, and thereby obtained the lease of the manor known as the 'Spittall', which was over the River Swift from Lutterworth, in the parish of Misterton, on the site of the ancient Hospital (hence its name) of St John the Baptist, endowed and consecrated in 1218 by Roaesia-de-Verdum, widow of the Lord of the Manor of Lutterworth. The estate was sequestrated by Queen Mary upon the execution in 1554 of the Duke of Suffolk (the father of Lady Jane Grey) into whose hands it had come. In the reign of Elizabeth I, the now ruined hospital was demolished and at some point the new manor built. Through marriage, however, the manor passed one generation later out of the Cole family to a Rev Bailey Shuttleworth and, together with the advowson, sold in 1776, but not before a descendant, one Robert Shuttleworth, had demanded the feudal right of compelling the inhabitants of Lutterworth to grind their corn at one of the estate's mills, which he burned down in pique when he lost his law-suit against the parishioners in 1758. The Coles, nonetheless, had remained in Lutterworth, actively

Early Days

supporting the Congregational Chapel, established in 1684, and producing the 'wollen manufacturer' Richard Cole, who was a founding member of the redoubtable Old Gooseberry Show Society. Necessarily bereft of historical documentation, there is a much earlier familial tradition that the Coles were descended from a descendant of the French knight Robert de Brus from Brix, namely Robert I the Bruce, king of the Scots (1306-1329), whose determination was legendarily of arachnid inspiration.

James and Ann King had eight children, of whom four died in infancy. The others were Annie Matilda, Emma, James (born on 3 May 1869, and also a Leicestershire cricketer) and John Herbert (often throughout his life called Jack outside the family) who was born in Lutterworth, like his siblings, on 16 April 1871.

Little can be ascertained now of John Herbert King's boyhood and youth. He sang in the choir of the parish church for eight years and both he and brother James were active as young boys, roaming the surrounding countryside and paddling and fishing in the River Swift, where in 1428 Wycliffe's ashes were cast after his disinterred remains had been burned as those of a heretic by a mob sent by the Bishop of Lincoln. Jack grew into a healthy lad, strong, vigorous, muscular, lean, lissom and tall (ultimately just over five feet eleven inches). In their teenage years they both attended, as boarders though they lived a scant half-mile way, Lutterworth Grammar School (more correctly named at the time the Sherrier School of the Foundation, and recently re-named Lutterworth College), which in later years produced two further cricketers of note for the county. One was Nigel Briers, the youngest player ever to represent Leicestershire, its captain for six years and later a teacher, at Ludgrove Preparatory School, of the royal princes William and Harry before he accepted a post at Marlborough College (where he had been preceded in 1899 by another Leicestershire player and occasional captain, the Cambridge Blue H.H.Marriott). The second was Nick Cook, who played with some distinction in nine Tests before moving to Northamptonshire.

King became an excellent sprinter and gained in stamina by accompanying his elder brother, a long-distance runner, on training runs from Lutterworth to Bitteswell and towards Leicester and back. But he was clearly a mischievous lad, on one early occasion playing truant from school to skate on Misterton Pool before the ice was thick enough to bear his weight. Met on the High

Street by his mother returning from chapel, the chilled and bedraggled miscreant urchin was hurried home and nursed for several weeks before fully recovering. In more organized sports he was to excel at boxing, fencing and especially as a three-quarter at rugby football.

According to his daughter he was first encouraged to concentrate on cricket by his headmaster, the Rev Robert Seddon, who used to place on each of his stumps a sixpenny piece (a princely sum at the time) to incite the bowling aspirations of his pupil, although at that time young Jack 'had some aptitude' also 'for keeping wicket'.[3] He clearly showed great promise early on, for when still a junior boy at the school he was given permission on one occasion at least to skip lessons in favour of playing for the town club. When King attended Lutterworth Grammar School it had few pupils. Though built in 1880 to accommodate 80, it had only 40 boys attending by 1885 and a mere 24 by 1889. It was closed between 1895 and 1898 – hence probably the lack of records before then. The school history by a former headmaster, George Irving, states that sporting activities of the early years are very difficult to trace as no magazines exist from before 1916. If there were any school matches in King's times, their flavour may perhaps be caught in the reminiscences in the *Lutterworthian* of 1953 by an old boy, J.H.Hubbard, who was at the school from 1898 to 1902, and wrote that 'Our greatest thrill at school was of course to get into the school cricket and football teams. Very many happy times we had, especially when we played away games against Hinckley GS, Loughborough GS and several schools in Leicester, especially the old Wyggeston boys, but we only played the second XI of the latter school. Each journey meant a four horse wagonette ride and a cheery sing song on the way home whether we won or lost.'

After his school-days had ended, King briefly entered the printing trade with a Mr F.W.Bottrill. He continued to play rugger and also boxed and fenced with Messrs W.G.Rose and J. and T.S.Smart, all fellow-members of the local rugby and cricket clubs. Notwithstanding his skill in these other sports, however, his greatest successes and enthusiasm indubitably involved cricket.

---

3 All quotations, unless otherwise attributed, are from the *Leicester Daily Mercury* (later simply *Leicester Mercury*).

Early Days

The Lutterworth Cricket Club has a long and honourable history. It may have come into existence only two years after the Marylebone Cricket Club, for there is record of a match between Lutterworth and neighbouring Ullesthorpe on 23 May 1789. Certainly it was in existence a few years later and in the middle and late nineteenth century was one of the most powerful in the county. King may have received hints here from the Rev Edward Elmhirst, rector of nearby Shawell, in whose garden Tennyson wrote parts of his *In Memoriam* – the rector had married a ward of the poet's father. For many years Elmhirst loyally supported the Lutterworth club, having a pavilion erected and surrounding seats provided, and coaching the players. By King's time, though, his contributions were probably limited in extent since he was 82 when he died in 1893. A batsman and wicket-keeper, his cricketing credentials were considerable, for in his prime he had been one of the most prominent players for the county club. Further afield he had represented Cambridge University in 1834, when there was no University match; the North; the Gentlemen, for whom as opening batsman in the winning match against the Players at Lord's in 1848 he was the only player on his side to reach double figures; and MCC. Between 1834 and 1853, he played in fifteen matches now recognized as first-class. It was said of Elmhirst that he would have been an archbishop if his preaching had been as good as his cricket.

Of more importance to King there were, still playing for the club or closely following its fortunes in retirement, three notable players. R.W.Gillespie-Stainton of Bitteswell Hall, just outside Lutterworth, had been in the Harrow XI of 1861 and a regular player for Leicestershire in the 1880s: he became a committee member of the county club when it was reformed in 1879. The Rev William Townshend had been in the Rossall XI, was an Oxford Blue (he had played in sixteen first-class matches for the University, including 'Cobden's Match' in 1870), had played for MCC and was only the second cricketer, after William Lambert, known to have scored two centuries in a match (for Rossall against the Old Boys in 1867). He had played for Leicestershire from 1881 to 1885 during his long rectorship of Thurlaston. Charles Marriott of Cotesbach Hall, two miles south of Lutterworth, the first member of his family to be a lay squire, was a J.P. and had been High Sheriff of Leicestershire in 1878. As a cricketer he was a Wykehamist and Oxford Blue who had played also for the Gentlemen of England, MCC (on whose committee he served several terms) and I Zingari, appearing in 31 first-class matches between 1870 and 1882. He had helped form the Leicester Cricket Association in 1873 and been the original vice-president of the county club in 1879, playing for the side for many years, together with two of his brothers, captaining it for six years and scoring its first-ever century, in 1883 against MCC at Lord's.

It was during this period, while he was playing for Lutterworth, that King became connected with the county club, for whom crucially Charles Marriott still occasionally played and whose president he was from 1890 to 1893. King was expected to join his father's building firm, but cricket's lure proved too strong, and instead of putting his eye to the plumb-line he would keep it on a ball; for during the summers he practised and received coaching at the County Ground, going the dozen or so miles in each direction on foot, but with a ball in hand to improve his catching and while away the tedium of an oft-repeated journey. Then 'one fine day', as 'Reynard' recalled years later in the *Leicester Daily Mercury*, 'some deliveries he sent along to Dick Pougher so impressed the renowned player that he recommended him to the County Committee'.

Three of the leading figures in nineteenth-century cricket in Lutterworth. Left to right: Rev Edward Elmhirst, Rev William Townshend, Charles Marriott.

Chapter Two
Apprenticeship

King first came before the public, to use the idiom of the day, in 1895, the year in which Leicestershire was admitted to the County Championship (although twelve of its county fixtures the previous year had been accepted as 'first-class'). He was paid £1 15s 0d a week for twenty weeks, a wage occasionally supplemented for him by a match fee.

The County Ground in 1895 was that now known as Grace Road but then as the Aylestone Ground, just off the main Lutterworth to Leicester road and about two miles south of the city centre. It was at the time not a famous ground, unlike a predecessor on Wharf Street, site in 1836 of the first 'home' match of the North v South and whence the triumphant Alfred Mynn was laid upon a stage-coach roof for the journey to London, so battered by Redgate's bowling that amputation of his right leg was feared. Nonetheless, Grace Road had witnessed in 1878 the first-ever century in England by an 'Australian', the Woolwich-born Charles Bannerman, when Leicestershire was the first county to offer the visitors a lump sum for playing; and Leicestershire's sensational defeat of the Australians ten years later, after which the professionals were presented with £5 each and the amateurs with engraved silver snuff-boxes. Although the ground is on slightly elevated land with a sharpish drop to the west and at the north-west corner, its drainage, until extensive work in the 1990s, was poor since it has a slight rise to the south and consists of Boulder Clay over Keuper Marl. Its pitch and outfield, moreover, were rough, a legacy of its earlier use as ploughed fields belonging to the Duke of Rutland. It was in consequence frequently not conducive to good batting, and it is hardly surprising that in the seven years of its first-class cricket before 1946 there were only two scores by home batsmen over 117. Nevertheless, Fred Root, the Derbyshire, Worcestershire and England professional, who was once on the Leicestershire staff and had gone to school only a few hundred yards away, claimed that it was 'one of the best grounds ever made'; but his youthful memories were probably enhanced by the fact that his father had been groundsman there for many years. Throughout King's time at Grace Road from 1895 to 1900 the wickets were pitched from east to west, parallel to the pavilion, rather than in their present, north-to-south alignment. Eric Snow writes that this was the case 'for a time', but perhaps it had been so ever since the ground was opened in 1878, for James King recalled being taken to see the Australians play that year and Spofforth bowling 'from the railway end', which must have been from the East.

The Grace Road ground in about 1890.

Among the four Colts to whom the county gave trials in 1895 were King and Albert Knight (two and a half years his junior), who became lifelong friends. Knight was tried first, in the second Championship and first home game of the season, a victory over Nottinghamshire. King was tried in the fourth match, against Essex, which began on 3 June, on which day the main news in Leicestershire was that a child had been run over at Moira by a horse, and nationally that Gladstone, who was celebrating the 62nd anniversary of his maiden speech in the Commons, 'although much better this morning, is confined to his room by a cold'. There was 'a large gathering of spectators in the pretty little ground at Leyton', but the pitch was, according to *Wisden*, 'fast and inclined to be fiery', enabling Harry Pickett to obtain statistically the greatest bowling performance ever suffered by Leicestershire, for he took all ten wickets at a cost of only 32 runs in a total of 111 (to improve on his previous best performance of just four for 6). King came in, before lunch on the first day, last but one, but 'shaped well' and battled his way to 12 to become the only player not dismissed by Pickett. His innings then proved more than the difference between the sides when Pougher and Woodcock routed Essex for 103. In his second innings King was bowled for three by the even more fearsome Kortright, who finished with eight wickets in his best return hitherto – eight for 63. In the last innings of the match King had his first bowl, a brief spell which included his first maiden, finishing with no wicket for ten; but his first catch (of a final total of 339, from the amateur G.F.Higgins) off Fred Geeson (who was still a fast bowler at that stage of his career before the condemnation of his action by the county captains) probably gave him some satisfaction in contributing to his county's victory by 75 runs.

The authorities were clearly encouraged by his performance since he was selected for the next match, at home against Yorkshire. In the first innings he was the last man in a hat-trick by Hirst (caught by the wicket-keeper), who then bowled him for nought in the second. He took no catch and was not needed to bowl, as Dick Pougher, whom King was destined to replace as Leicestershire's premier all-rounder, took 12 wickets. He played only two further matches, appearing together with Knight for the first time at Sheffield, where he followed a not out two with another duck against Hirst (lbw this time), and suffering two ducks at Edgbaston. Hirst was certainly to prove his bête-noire, dismissing him many times including for 'spectacles' again on a 'hideous' pitch at Hull in 1907, where King was the middle victim this time of another hat-trick remarkable in that, since the other victims were Wood and Knight, Hirst clean bowled Leicestershire's three best batsmen in three balls. King never completely fathomed the Yorkshireman, who inflicted further 'spectacles' on him in a match against MCC as late as 1912.[4]

King's batting average for the season was thus 2.83, with five ducks in his last six innings, a dismal record even when one considers that two of his four matches were against Yorkshire and that against Essex on a bad wicket. In bowling he had failed to take a wicket for the 62 runs conceded. Was he, despite his natural ability, too nervous, allowing failure to prey upon him? Knight, who far more easily and at a younger age made the transition to first-class cricket, may have had his friend in mind when, on 13

---

[4] In all Hirst dismissed King 20 times, a figure second only to Rhodes' 23 times, but, unlike his fellow-Yorkshireman, Hirst bowled very seldom in the last seven years of King's career.

August 1904, he wrote in the *Leicester Daily Mercury*: 'Looking across the lapse of years in manhood's misty light it seems almost impossible to realize that one's first matches should have affected one as they did. One now sees the real worth or insignificance of them, how little we ought to permit them to trouble us, but the sad heart of the unsuccessful colt of to-day and his inability to receive consolation, at the best "wearing a face of joy" when smiles are far away, is a visible symbol of inarticulate feeling never wholly outgrown, though less palpable and defined in later years. It is this nervousness and the heavy feeling of wandering about in some strange twilight land which terribly handicaps the young player, and which, if you have any faith in his ability at all, necessitates trusting him to long experience as absolutely necessary 'ere he begins to realize himself and his powers.'

Meanwhile something clearly had to be done if King wished to pursue a career as a professional cricketer. He was already 24 and his father, who wished him to enter the family's building firm, could not support him indefinitely.

He was fortunate in obtaining an engagement as professional at Birkenhead Park, a rich club of exclusively ex-public-school men when founded in 1846 (the first in the Wirral) and able to employ professionals to do the 'manual work' of bowling to members in the nets. Long before 1896, however, a major function of these professionals had come to be playing in matches. How King came to obtain a position is unknown to-day. In his time it was the club's habit to write to Lord Hawke for a recommendation, but the Yorkshire captain was hardly likely to have known King well enough. The most suasive hypothesis is that his name was suggested by Edwin Smith who had been born at Peatling Magna, between Lutterworth and Leicester, in 1860, first played for Leicestershire in 1883 and become professional at Birkenhead the following year, thus qualifying by residence for Cheshire (for whom he scored a century against his native county). Smith, according to Birkenhead's historian Chris Elston, 'is said to have been the best fast bowler the club ever had' and was one of its professionals for the whole of King's stint there, retiring home to Leicestershire only after his benefit year of 1899.[5] Another possibility is that King was recommended to the post by the

---

5   Liverpool and District played fourteen first-class matches between 1882 and 1894; Smith played in nine of these, his entire first-class career, taking 25 wickets at 19.48.

famous Arnold ('Bobby') Rylott, a fast left round-arm bowler who had been professional in Birkenhead for a few years from 1867 (twice being primarily responsible for victories over the All England Eleven) before giving sterling service to Leicestershire from 1873 to 1890 in pre-first-class days. Factors suggesting Rylott's involvement are that he was a senior member of the ground staff at Lord's,[6] which King joined in 1899 directly after leaving Birkenhead, and that the club's minute book has an entry for 1898 to the effect that the club captain Cecil Holden had written unsuccessfully to both Smith and Rylott enquiring about a possible replacement for King.

Arnold Rylott, professional cricketer and poet, had a hand in King's early career.

King's weekly wage, at least in his first year, was £2 15s 0d, of which the club, no longer rich, paid £2 5s 0d, the remaining ten shillings being made good by the members who were charged an additional one shilling each for the season. This arrangement by which the club itself paid only part of his salary was continued, for the minute book records that for the following season 'the secretary was instructed to do his utmost to secure guarantors towards the wages of King so as to lessen the amount of the indebtedness of the club'. It is perhaps indicative of his scanty credentials that the professional whom he replaced, Ellis Town, despite the fact that he had been given a 'final warning' over inebriation three years before, had been employed at the rate of £3 per week.[7]

Although King's contract no longer exists, it was almost certainly the standard contract of Birkenhead Park, which contained the following three clauses:

> 1. The said — shall be employed by and shall act as Professional Cricketer, Groundsman and Coach to the said Club from — to — .

---

6   Rylott, born in Lincolnshire in 1839, played in 85 first-class matches between 1870 and 1888, of which 72 were for MCC. Leicestershire awarded him a benefit in 1888.

7   Town, born at Halifax in 1866, never played first-class cricket. He played one match in the Minor Counties championship, for Cheshire in 1895, scoring six runs and taking four wickets.

2. As such professional cricketer and coach as aforesaid his duties amongst others shall be those of playing in matches – bowling at practice nets – preparing wickets for matches and practice and generally performing the customary and proper duties of a professional cricketer and groundsman.

3. In consideration of the premises and the said — well and faithfully performing his said duties the said Club agree to pay him the sum of — per week during the period aforesaid.

King's duties included also umpiring in games played by the club's second team. The professionals did not have much time in which to prepare the pitches before the season commenced, being, in 1896 for instance, required 'to commence work on 18 April' before the first home match on 2 May. Despite misgivings, remarkable for the period, among some members, he and his fellow-professional Edwin Smith, when playing themselves, had to enter the field separately from the amateurs, emerging from one side of the ladies' pavilion, which was later converted into a still-existent stand. The main pavilion of the club, brick-built in 1849, is certainly the oldest on Merseyside and has some claim to be the oldest in the country.

During his inaugural season of 1896, King played 25 matches under the captaincy of Cecil Holden between 2 May and 31 August, bowling in all and batting in all but three. Since playing at New Brighton or Rock Ferry in one-day matches was a far cry from facing Hirst at Bramall Lane in a three-day match, success at this level was absolutely essential for any return to higher pastures. He was undoubtedly a success in bowling, ending with 63 wickets at an average of 16.73 with a best return of seven for 18 against Sefton Park and six wickets in an innings thrice, including once against that marvellously named team *Hoi Pepneumenoi* (which can be translated as 'The Wise' and also 'The Still Breathing'), and once against Manchester C.C. in a match in which King and his fellow Leicestershire colleague Edwin Smith took all ten wickets between them. In batting, however, he continued a tendency to fail to score (six times out of 22 innings), had a highest score of only 32* and an average, bolstered by seven not outs, of only 17.13. In the friendly match against Leicester Ivanhoe, which he may have arranged, he took only one for 57 and did not bat. His county did not see fit to give him any matches; Knight, though, was now beginning to make a name for himself, finishing second in the county batting averages to Pougher.

Birkenhead Park was barely satisfied with his performances, initially passing a unanimous resolution to dispense with his services, a sub-committee being 'formed to look at the question of filling the vacancy on the ground staff', on which the captain Holden applied to Hawke for advice. Notwithstanding, the club eventually engaged him for the following season, and was rewarded by an improved record in both principal departments. His bowling was magnificent – 92 wickets at an average of 11.69, with a best performance of nine for 33 against Leyland when he took the first nine to fall; and he twice took seven, twice six, four times five and five times four wickets in only 22 innings, in none of which he failed to dismiss at least one opponent. His batting average, despite being nearly twice as high as his bowling, 23.00 for 368 runs, was not a huge improvement on the previous season, although his runs did include five innings superior to his previous season's best, one of which was a magnificent 100 not out against New Brighton, the first by a professional for the club, when his seven for 82 gave him an outstanding match-double.

Meanwhile Leicestershire was not enjoying a happy season. On 16 August there appeared a satirical piece in the *Leicester Daily Mercury*: 'When the county cricket history of the present year of grace comes to be written nothing will be more remarkable... than the splendid consistency of the Leicestershire eleven. What matters it to Leicestershire whether the wicket be fast or slow, the weather wet or fine, their opponents weak or strong? "Our" cricketers... hold a conceited sort of disregard for the traditional uncertainty of the summer pastime, and have bravely set themselves out to prove one thing – that the result of a county match is a foregone conclusion when Leicestershire is one of the teams actively engaged. This course of action has its advantages. Close followers of the county, and local enthusiasts – if there are any left – are spared the suspense of waiting to the end of a match before knowing the result, and spectators at their various games stand in no fear of an attack of heart disease through the excitement of a close finish.'

It is not surprising, then, that King was called up midway through the summer; and in his first match, against Warwickshire at Grace Road, he top-scored for his side with his first half-century (56), 'display[ing] more confidence than the majority' of his team-mates. He was given the brunt of the bowling too and, despite the fact that he took none for 129 in Warwickshire's then record score of 472, his 14 maidens out of 54 overs indicated a promising steadiness. For the next match, against Derbyshire, he shot up the order, from No.8 to No.4, and a couple of twenties showed his new confidence and helped his county to its solitary victory of the season. In a further three matches he achieved little, but had the satisfaction of taking his first wicket, having G.R.Baker caught by C.J.B.Wood at Old Trafford, a ground with which he was familiar from two matches with Birkenhead Park. The *Leicester Daily Mercury* opined that it was 'long overdue'. King's batting average had now jumped to 16.90, which was much better than it sounds, for Knight was top with only 20.00 in a summer of variable weather which on only rare occasions justified the contemporary advertisement of Brooke Bond's tea as the beverage for 'the sultry summer afternoon'.

Leicestershire's side of 1897 was thirteenth of fourteen in the Championship. Standing (l to r): W.Tomlin, A.Woodcock, F.Geeson and J.H.King. Seated: C.J.B.Wood, F.W.Stocks, C.E.de Trafford (captain), A.D.Pougher and A.E.Knight. On the ground: J.P.Whiteside (wk) and S.Coe.

Birkenhead Park was, understandably, in no doubt about engaging him for a third season, and despite a slight slip in batting average to 20.30 he once more excelled in bowling with 77 wickets at 12.71, making Ormskirk in particular suffer with eight for 40 and eight for 20 in the two games. He further enjoyed himself in the sort of match beloved by the Victorians with a score of 76 and a return of six for 92 for the Single against the Married. More important, however, was his first 'proper' representative match, not however first-class, for Liverpool and District against Cambridge University at Aigburth in July. Batting at No.8 in both innings he scored 27 out of 399 in the first innings and a very valuable 38 out of a mere 172 in the second. Although unsuccessful with nought for 16 in the University's first innings of 290, he took three for 26 on the last day, his disappointment at just failing to bring his side victory (Cambridge held out with one wicket to fall and 79 runs to score) perhaps partly palliated by catching, off his own bowling, the redoubtable Gilbert Jessop, then in the first of his glorious years of unparalleled fast scoring.

Interest continued to be taken in him by Leicestershire, which had recently engaged as coach the ebullient Yorkshireman Tom Emmett, who proved an excellent choice with a wealth of experience, having played 298 matches for Yorkshire between 1866 and 1888 (as captain for five years) and seven for England and toured both Australia and North America. He was an inspirational coach with no fancy airs – he had turned up for his first professional engagement in clogs and with his kit wrapped up in a newspaper – and, as a left-handed all-rounder, he was especially helpful to King until his death in 1904.

Despite playing only six matches for his county, King increased his seasonal aggregate to 242 runs, which for ten dismissals placed him fourth in the county averages and above Knight, who again played regularly. He also at last gave a glimpse in first-class cricket of his bowling prowess, increasing his career total of two wickets by a multiple of six and conceding only 277 runs off 128.4 overs for his ten wickets. He achieved various personal milestones: a highest score of 77 against Middlesex, when he batted at a new high of No.3 and 'made some splendid hits' (especially off-drives), followed by a half-century notable for its freedom in cutting in his very next innings; opening the bowling and taking three wickets, both for the first time, against Surrey at Leicester and achieving his best figures with three for 43 at The Oval. What probably gave him most satisfaction, however, was a return of three for 88 out of a total of 449 against Yorkshire at Leicester, since his victims were the redoubtable trio of Tunnicliffe, F.S.Jackson and Lord Hawke; he also had Denton missed off a 'fairly easy chance' by Woodcock. For the first time *Wisden* sees fit to make mention of him (with its notorious dislike of commas): 'It seemed that another reliable bat had been found in King. Tried occasionally in 1897 he played in most of the matches up to the middle of July but after scoring 77 against Middlesex and 50 against Surrey he was not again seen in the field. For eleven innings he had an average of 24 so that his services could ill be spared.' His local newspaper percipiently saw much promise in him and other youngsters: 'Some of the present members of the Leicestershire eleven will be playing – aye, and making centuries – when many of their present opponents have been relegated to the ease and serenity of the umpire's smock, or are enjoying the placid air of the pavilion'.

For the following year he was again re-engaged (together with Edwin Smith) by Birkenhead Park even before the 1898 season was over; but we must assume that he had received at least encouraging comments by his county, for Birkenhead Park's minute book has an entry for late August that reads: 'The secretary was instructed to write to King and inform him that the committee while accepting his resignation would be pleased to give him any reference he might require'. In 1899 he became at last, at the age of 28, a regular for his county: his apprenticeship was over, his persistence rewarded, his father's doubts assuaged. But before we trace his career further we should consider what manner of player he was.

Chapter Three
Technique and Style

King was of a rare breed, a successful double-left-handed all-rounder.[8] There are only four such who have scored 10,000 (all actually over 20,000) runs and taken 1,000 wickets in the County Championship. Besides King there are John Gunn of Nottinghamshire, Frank Woolley of Kent and James Langridge of Sussex.[9] All four were middle-order batsmen and slow or medium-paced (or both with the exception of Langridge) bowlers. Since Gunn's career spanned almost exactly the same years as King's, occasional comparisons with him are made in this chapter. If account is taken of the fact that Gunn played for a far stronger team, and thus had much better support, it can be said that Gunn

---

8   A natural left-hander will automatically throw by preference with his left arm, and as a consequence the very first time he tries to perform the skill, will bowl left-arm too. He will also probably put his left hand below his right when holding a bat since his instinct will be to hit the ball in the air with a cross-bat to his right side, which is easier to accomplish if the stronger and more 'dexterous' hand is nearer the splice. Cricket is, however, a perverse and unnatural hitting game in that for nearly all strokes the ball should be kept on the ground. To achieve this, the upper arm, significantly called the leading arm, is of more importance. This should be obvious as any competent batsman who is forced by injury to play with only one hand, especially when the situation calls for an emphasis upon correct cricket rather than the scoring of a quick couple of fours, will use his able arm as the leading arm with corresponding stance even if that is contrary to his custom. Since, however, the grip with the left hand lower on the handle is called that of the left-hander, almost all parents of naturally left-handed children will not direct their children to hold the bat with the left hand above the right (and, of course, vice-versa for natural right-handers). It is idle to speculate how many players, King included, would have been more proficient batsmen if guided in infancy to hold their bats the right way for playing cricket strokes rather than in accordance with the terminology of 'right-handed' and 'left-handed' batsmen. To change in later boyhood or at an even higher age is hard. Sadiq Mohammad, it is said, was persuaded by brother Hanif to change because Pakistan lacked a 'left-handed' batsman, but, since Hanif (though far from a regular bowler) is reputed to have bowled left and right in two first-class matches, there was probably ambidexterity in the family.

9   The two great Yorkshire left-arm bowlers Hirst and Rhodes batted right. Of Leicestershire all-rounders (with generous application of the term) only King, Coe, Walsh and Munden were double-left-handers, but Pougher, Wood, Astill, Geary, Shipman (A.W.), Lester, Jackson, Palmer, van Geloven, Knight (B.R.), Marner, Illingworth, Clift, McVicker, de Freitas, Lewis, Simmons, Maddy, Wells and Kasprowicz were double-right-handers. It is perhaps significant that the only all-rounders who, according to the traditional description, batted one way and bowled the other have been of recent vintage: Lock, Steele, Balderstone, Potter and Henderson were or are right-handed batsmen and left-arm bowlers, Birkenshaw, Millns, Parsons and Dakin left-handed batsmen and right-arm bowlers.

was a somewhat better bat, though a failure in his six Test matches, and that King was a somewhat better bowler, despite a very slightly inferior average.[10]

No moving film of King exists. Beldam and Fry, however, chose fortunately for us to illustrate technique with four photographs of him as batsman and four as bowler. Chevallier Tayler furthers slightly our study of him in the former rôle since his chalk drawing on dark grey paper, probably based upon one of Beldam's unpublished photographs, shows a position mid-way between the third and fourth of those in *Great Batsmen: their Methods at a Glance* but with front toe raised. Such dependence would not be surprising since prints of Tayler's 48 drawings of cricketers first appeared in weekly parts put out by the Art Society in 1905, the

Compare and contrast.
On the left, Knight's rigidity leaves a bat/pad gap: King's stance has a more 'modern' relaxed approach.

---

10 In all first-class matches Gunn scored 24,557 runs, with 40 centuries, at an average of 33.18 and took 1,242 wickets at an average of 24.52. He held 246 catches.

Technique and Style

year of publication of that book, before being combined in a single volume with commentary by none other than Beldam. A fifth photograph of King at Birkenhead shows his stance. Other photographs of him as a bowler are all posed and of no additional help. With such paucity of visual evidence we are forced to rely largely on written evidence.

King was well built, nearly six feet in height and with a long reach. He was, moreover, at least in his prime, lean rather than thin, extremely athletic, lissom, swift of foot and of quick reaction. His courage, even in old age, was not to be doubted, however much he was on occasion bruised.

Chevallier Taylor's chalk drawing probably derives from photographs taken by G.W.Beldam.

As a batsman he was correct and orthodox with a good defence and aggressive scoring strokes – *Wisden* of 1901 claims that he was 'of the hard-hitting school' – and most effective in both modes against fast bowling. In his stance his left foot was behind and parallel with the crease, right heel partly behind the crease with toes pointing diagonally in front, bat sloping into the body in contradistinction with the more old-fashioned straight bat favoured by his colleague Knight. His whole stance gives an impression of watchfulness and readiness to move into any position for defence or attack.

In his formative years, with the general improvement of wickets after the middle of the century, forward play was the norm. Indeed, as late as March 1924, *The Cricketer* published a poem by Edward G.Evans, prefaced by a perverse adaptation of lines in Horace's sixth Roman ode[11] worthy of Pycroft or Felix, on the sad fate of an imaginary prep-school lad named Peter Barlow Jones

---

11   Odes 3.6.37-41

who favoured playing back. It ends with the headmaster's term report and the moral:

> Of Peter candidly I say – ability quite good,
> There must be mathematical corpuscles in his blood;
> His common sense is excellent; I've never known him slack:
> But ruin stares him in the face, because he WILL PLAY BACK!

> No doubt high honour beckons him to lesser spheres of fame,
> In scientific circles his will be a laurelled name;
> But yet the topmost rung of glory must his presence lack,
> And this his epitaph, "He failed, because he WOULD PLAY BACK."

> Lay this to heart, you Prep. School boys, lest worse should you befall,
> And throw your left foot forward to the pitching of the ball.
> If you play back, a time will come when you will be too late,
> And then, which Heav'n forbid, you'll suffer Rachel's awful fate!

King first learned his cricket in the late 1870s and the 1880s, and at the Lutterworth club will have been advised by the Rev Edward Elmhirst, an apostle of forward play. At Leicester his captain was Charles de Trafford, an extraordinarily aggressive hitter who excelled at the drive, once with this stroke scoring a boundary off a bare knuckle in his contempt of batting gloves. From 1895, when King made his county début, until 1904 the Leicestershire coach was the popular and irrepressible Tom Emmett, of whom Albert Knight writes that he had 'an almost exclusive attachment to' what was then called the 'push stroke'. 'Nothing pleased him more than its good execution'. This stroke was a sort of gentle drive, the front foot advanced close to the line of the ball, the front shoulder and elbow kept forward over the ball and the weight of the body transferred to the front foot at the moment of impact; but there was often little back-lift or follow-through and, crucially, the lower hand was dominant. It was played both defensively and offensively. Knight adds that 'Many a player in first-class cricket gets forties and fifties with no other stroke than this when wickets are uniform and fast'.

King was inevitably an adept at this 'push stroke', which Fry disdains on the grounds, *inter alia*, that it is weaker than the drive, is not as safe as even 'half-cock play' and is never necessary. King clearly weaned himself from over-reliance on this stroke, for he indubitably favoured the drive, which was in his day still the noblest, most gallant, indeed the most chivalrous and gentlemanly stroke; and his most commonly used drive was the most splendid of all, that through the covers, although he had the full range from that forward of point through the straight to that forward of square leg. His straight drives, however, were usually just to off or on, and he was not deprived of many runs by the opposing stumps, as was to be Maurice Tompkin in later years. In driving he was aided by a very muscular leading (right) fore-arm, as can be seen below in the first of Beldam's photographs of him bowling; and he frequently ran yards down the pitch to play the stroke (even occasionally at the age of 54), although, fortunately, learning to curb his impetuosity somewhat after having been stumped three times already by mid-June in 1900 through jumping out of his crease. During his whole career he was stumped 39 times in all, which accounts for 4.2% of his dismissals. This percentage would be considered high to-day, when some county wicket-keepers go through a whole season without stumping a single batsman, but was not in his time (Gunn's percentage is 7.2). The comparatively low figure is testament to his hard-learned restraint and even more to his fine eye.

Beldam's photographs of him batting are of four stages in his off-drive, which Fry uses to illustrate the second of his three categories of this stroke, the 'off-drive with right [it would have been better if he had used 'back' to accommodate left-handers such as King] foot firm before impact, but allowed to move up in the follow-through'. It must be emphasized that since Beldam, the pioneer in photography of cricketers in action rather than posing, did not have the equipment to take pictures in rapid succession, the four photographs are not of King's response to the same ball but to four different balls; the first two were well outside the line of the off stump, the latter two much nearer in line to it. The third with closed face of bat and right elbow tucked into side (which would have caused him to play across the line) suggests that the ball in this case was not suitable for the off-drive, which King had been told to perform. Notably the bat is far more open-faced in Tayler's drawing of a fractionally later moment in the same phase of the stroke. To take the positions in sequence, the first photograph shows the bat almost horizontal in the down-swing with the head and torso leaning forward, the right foot already on the ground far forward to the off, the left toe dragged just in front of the popping crease. In the second the left foot is almost vertical on the toe as the batsman leans over the ball (though perhaps not

Technique and Style

Beldam's action photographs help us to analyse some aspects of King's technique.

Technique and Style

quite as much as Tom Emmett would have liked with his much reiterated 'smell 'er'). The third shows the position just after impact, the back foot now well over the popping crease, although that foot is in this picture not as near the vertical owing to the position of the front foot between middle and off rather than well outside off stump. In the fourth photograph the bat is at its height in the follow-through, the batsman's body completely and strikingly upright, whereas Beldam's illustrations of other batsmen at the conclusion of this stroke all show some degree of forward inclination until the bat is almost horizontal behind the batsman's back. The variation in position of the front foot, the heel ranging from just on the leg side of middle stump to well outside off, was determined of course by the width of the ball. Clearly he put his foot well to the line of the ball, thus leaving little gap between bat and pad and not feeding the slips with an uncontrolled prod. A further observation can be made from these photographs: King's bottom hand is very close to the splice, indicating that he tended to use it too much in the production of, especially, attacking forward strokes.[12]

King was an excellent forward-player, like so many batsmen of his era, a consequence of both his upbringing and the type of ball he most often faced, for until the outbreak of the Great War, and even for some years thereafter, bowlers, by employing a fairly full length, to a considerable extent accommodated forward play. Nevertheless, as Fry remarks, the opening years of the twentieth century, early in which King passed into his thirties, witnessed the growth of 'skilful and scientific . . . back play', which Fry opines is 'even more important than forward play' especially on turning wickets. Even earlier in his book dedicated to 'The Queen-Empress' Ranjitsinhji (or was it already Fry?) had emphasized, against prevailing opinion, the importance of playing back as being safer than playing forward when 'part of the stroke is made on faith', a quotation picked up by D.L.A.Jephson in his advice in the 1904 *Wisden*: 'when in doubt play back, and *keep on playing back*' (Jephson's italics). Herein Knight, who first played for his county in the same year as King and therefore was under the same tutelage of Tom Emmett for seven years, concurs: 'These back-play strokes need a very watchful eye, yet there is no method of play in which

---

12   This also could have been a contributory cause of the closed face in the third photograph. Perhaps when a young boy he should have been encouraged, since he was naturally left-handed, to bat the other way round so that his leading arm would have been his stronger left.

the boy who desires to excel should more carefully train himself. ... The player of beyond average skill has been in all times a great back player.' King clearly learned to play off the back foot with consummate skill and grammatical correctness in defence as well as in attack, in the former becoming adept especially in defending against fast-rising balls on crumbled, sticky and also just slow wickets. Whether his cuts, for which he was famous, were made by a forward or lateral movement of his front leg or a back or lateral movement of his back leg I can, unfortunately, find no evidence to show, nor whether he employed the so-called 'forward cut', which Fry classifies rather as a square off-drive, forcing back stroke or 'a species of slash'. Newspaper reports, unfortunately, regularly refer simply to 'cuts' and 'cutting'; but one already in 1901 mentions his late-cut at which he became very proficient. The photographs of him batting and especially the first of him bowling show exceptionally muscular forearms which, combined, with his powerful wrists enabled him to make firm cuts which frequently were kept low, although on occasion were lofted, once even for six, an event far less common then than with the heavier bats in the tumultuous and at times Bedlamite exuberance of modern one-day cricket.

Even though no longer in King's time was a ball to the leg deemed the delivery of a cad or incompetent and worthy of an apology from the perpetrator, yet the 'Golden Age' showed a distinct preference for the off-side; and King, as we have seen, was an adept at off-side strokes. Notwithstanding, he soon developed leg-side strokes: indeed, one South African newspaper, in introducing him to its readership in 1905, writes, 'He bats left-handed, and like most of his Benjamite brethren, is terribly strong on the leg side'. A later report notes that 'his leg strokes [were] forceful and very neatly timed'. In addition to strong on-driving we may note that in the first decade of the century, when he was at his full strength and still with very swift reactions, he could hook with great power; and the stroke is still mentioned in reports of his batting in 1925. He employed also the pull or pulled drive, which the archetypical flouter of conventions Edward Mills Grace, with his marvellous eye-and-wrist co-ordination, had perfected but Fry considered a dangerous stroke, and which Ranjitsinhji claimed 'should be' only 'a manner of dealing with a very easy ball, or a ball that had been made very easy by the batsman's judgment'. Certainly on the uncovered wickets of 'The Coroner's' day such a cross-batted stroke was usually to be eschewed. Newspapers also advert, again as early as 1901, to King's leg-glances, which seem to have been, as with most batsmen including Ranjitsinhji, more forcing strokes to leg than mere angled glides. As King aged he became more of a back-foot and leg-side player. In comparing his controlled classicism with the boisterous rusticity of his slightly younger contemporary and fellow left-hander Sam Coe, *Wisden* writes of their batting in 1914: 'Coe, the more powerful in his methods, excelled in the off-drive which sent the ball with great force along the ground, the square cut and the lusty on-drive. King, fond of waiting for the ball, cut late, pulled, and used the leg glance in his more up-to-date style'. Even later, in the appreciation of King on the front page of the issue of *The Cricketer* for 16 July in its inaugural year of 1921, the writer (surely Pelham Warner) remarks that while 'he has all the left-hander's strokes on the off-side, [he] is particularly effective in persuading balls away to leg'. Notwithstanding, he never lost in any way his love for the drive. An old Leicestershire habitué and erstwhile committee member once told me that in the 1930s he had seen a gentleman in a blue serge suit spanking the bowling on the practice pitch with clean, crisp drives. This was King, then a venerable sixty-odd years old.

He seems, therefore, to have had the full repertoire of orthodox attacking strokes at his command; and in this he was aided by use of a bat perhaps a little on the heavy side even for his strong and muscular frame: that from 1904 now in the possession of his grand-daughter weighs, in its present completely dried state, 2lb 6¾oz. His friend Albert Knight preferred a slightly lighter implement and terms the 2lb 10oz weapon of the 'mere hitter' Albert Trott, as 'a savage beast of a thing', approving of 'gentler souls who can tap more effectively with a bat of 2lb 2oz.' What indeed would they have said of the railway-sleeper with which Graham Gooch scored a triple century against India in 1990 or, from a quite different period, William Ward's four-pound monster?

Despite his fondness for aggressive stroke-play King was certainly a thinking batsman, with not only the technical ability but also the patience to defend, sometimes for many hours, when the situation demanded, as it often did, for during most of his career Leicestershire had but a weak team and never seriously challenged for the Championship. His friend Knight described him in the local newspaper in 1904 as 'one of the most dogged and imperturbable of players . . . absolutely impervious to and undisturbed by any criticism, he is never more cool and level-headed than when conditions tend towards excitability'. The list of his long defensive innings is great, but he did on occasion forgo his legendary imperturbability, as for instance in his innings of 167 against Derbyshire in 1903, when the *Leicester Daily Mercury* reports that he 'practically stood still between 90 and 100. This fact seemed to suddenly dawn upon him, and with a do or die sort of an effort he smote out with might and main, and with a thud the ball fell inside the small stand'. Perhaps this was unfair criticism, or he later grew out of such madcap impetuosity; but, as was observed nigh on two decades later, he was the sort of batsman 'who in the worst conditions always believed that a little resolute hitting is worth while'.

How good was King defensively? It is, of course, much harder to learn of his defensive than of his offensive technique, for newspaper reporters reflect their readers' preference for accounts of derring-do, and Beldam and Fry did not choose him as an example for 'back play' or the defensive 'push stroke'. This much is clear: that his many innings with back to the wall prove considerable ability and self-discipline especially against fast bowling; and that he was a fair judge of which away-swinging balls to leave, competent in playing forward to scotch spin and increasingly proficient and eager to play back watchfully with a straight bat. Although it is impossible to ascertain how frequently King was caught in the slips, the fact that only 14.4% of his caught dismissals were by wicket-keepers[13] (Gunn's figure is 18.6%) may suggest that many of his catches were in the outfield off aggressive strokes, rather than results of a defective defensive technique. Perhaps his frequent dismissals bowled (35.8% of his total dismissals against Gunn's much lower 28.4%) but his fairly low percentage for lbw (7.3%) may also indicate rather an attacking spirit than poor defence.[14]

As was natural with a sprinter, he was a fast runner between the wickets – all-run fives are mentioned in reports – but his native caution inhibited the stealing of many runs. Comments such as,

---

13   That is by the known wicket-keeper: there may have been other occasions. The same proviso applies to Gunn's figures.
14   Dismissal lbw was, of course, much rarer before the change in the law in 1937 that allowed balls pitched outside the off stump to gain the verdict. Significantly, I think, King's figure of 7.3%, though only 0.8% lower than Gunn's 8.1%, is as much as 1.8% lower than the percentage of the times that King himself dismissed a batsman thus (9.1%).

Technique and Style

again from 1903, 'King foolishly ran himself out in attempting the impossible', are rare. In all he was run out 23 times, that is on average only once a season, a very low figure accounting for 2.5% of his dismissals.[15] There were occasions, when runs were unimportant but staying in was essential to stave off defeat, that he turned down easy runs to the frustration of his partners, not to mention the spectators. Needless to say, when he was in his fifties his running had appreciably slowed, and in his monumental 205 against Hampshire at the age of 52 there was not a single three.

Since nobody alive to-day saw King bat in his prime and there survives no detailed analysis of his batting and but four photographs, it is somewhat hazardous to assess him stylistically. In the feature on our cricketer which graced the front page of an edition of *The Cricketer* in 1921, it is averred that he 'is one of those left-handed batsmen who may be described as "busy"', but by that time he was already fifty years old (the writer makes an error of over two years in his date of birth). As has already been noted, he developed slowly and it was only when he was already in his thirtieth year that the local newspaper saw fit to announce that 'he seems to have lost the cramped and one-stroke style which previously characterised his play, and to have developed a much freer game'. Of him in his prime, the terms we read most often for his batting are 'free-swinging', 'free-flowing', 'powerful', 'correct', 'clean', 'crisp', 'flashing', 'graceful' and the less specific 'attractive'. These apply especially to his driving, notably into the covers, and cutting; but at times, with strokes to leg, the epithet is 'pretty'. Perhaps we can say, in architectural terms, that he was somewhat roughly sculpted Ionic, as opposed, amongst his colleagues, to the Doric C.J.B.Wood and the Corinthian C.E.de Trafford.[16] Could we perhaps describe the batsman King at his best as a sort of minor and somewhat less graceful because more pugnacious but still very attractive Graeme Pollock? Nevertheless, on occasion and to some eyes, his batting was too robust to be described as Ionic, 'J.C.' of the *Sporting Chronicle* giving him at Lord's in 1909 a quarterstaff in contrast with Hobbs' rapier.

Of King as a bowler we again have four action photographs from

---

15   Gunn's too was low at 2.7%.
16   Since my early years I have visualized an analogy between the Greek orders and batsmen's styles: perhaps I can make this analogy clearer with more recent examples – Cowdrey was Doric *in excelsis*, Dexter Corinthian, May Ionic, or, to give Leicestershire parallels for the Ionic, Hallam and Gower.

Beldam,[17] showing him wearing a cap. This was not uncommon for the period, and as fast a bowler as King's younger colleague George Geary was always thus attired even when in full flow. The photographs of his action may be supplemented by verbal reports which speak of it in terms such as 'beautifully easy'.

Contemporary reports sometimes call him a slow or slow-medium bowler, but in Beldam's and Fry's magisterial tome he is classified as a 'medium pace bowler' alongside, amongst others, Alec Hearne, Schofield Haigh, J.N.Crawford, Walter Mead, Arthur Hallam and Hugh Trumble, and thus faster than his fellow left-armers Wilfred Rhodes, Colin Blythe and James Hallows who are all categorized therein as 'slow medium'. These terms should probably not be taken as meaning quite the same then as to-day in an era of quickened 'slow' bowlers. Fry comments on his lack of a follow-through, which suggests no excessive pace. The first photograph, showing him in an extraordinarily upright posture some two or three strides from delivery and just before the transference of the ball from right to left hand, suggests that many antecedent steps would have been supererogatory – in old age he was described as taking a 'three-pace shuffle'. Nonetheless, he did enjoy opening the bowling and having the use of a hard ball, which, on a hard wicket and allied with his height and the fact that he kept his left arm high in delivery (even, as Philip Snow recalls, in old age) could give him uncomfortable lift,[18] although Fry, in speaking of spin on a sticky wicket, somewhat surprisingly claims that despite his high arm 'the ball after leaving his hand behaves very much as though delivered by a round-arm bowler of the old-fashioned kind'.

Like many slowish bowlers, he did have a faster delivery. Fry claims that his 'best point' was 'the skilful way in which he leads up to' this. It was achieved 'with his arm a little lower than usual ...

---

17   There are three other still extant photographs of King bowling, but these are all 'posed' and offer us little help. One photograph has him against an odd 'gardenly' background; another appeared in *The Cricketer* in 1921; the third in his 1923 benefit brochure.
18   Before the Second World War a slow bowler frequently opened an innings, and the combination of a fast and a slow bowler often had the advantage of unsettling the batsmen since they were not permitted to become accustomed to a single pace. In favourable conditions even the very slow bowler 'Tich' Freeman used to open the bowling for Kent. One of the most famous examples of this combination starting an innings occurred in the First Test of the 1909 series against Australia when Hirst and Blythe, in taking all 20 wickets between them (11 by Blythe) on a sodden pitch at Edgbaston, were primarily responsible for England's comfortable victory. Even opening with two slow bowlers was not uncommon; and we shall see that King and Astill often opened the bowling together for their native county.

[the ball] comes across quickly from the off and is inclined to keep rather low. Although he alters his action for this ball he does it so quickly towards the finish of the swing that the batsman is unprepared for it.'

In common with many of his left-arm colleagues of the time he bowled round the wicket; and just prior to delivery his position was very side-on, his shoulders arched backwards and his leading foot planted wide of the rear foot and as close to the return crease as possible. Even after delivery the left shoulder, as shown in the third photograph, had not come round very much. The final stage of his run-up was apparently very slightly diagonal, but, far more important, the resultant ball, since it started from well outside the line of wicket to wicket, came in to the right-handed batsman at an angle that it made it necessary for him to be extremely careful not to play outside it. If the ball did not deviate in line, it was next to impossible to win an appeal for lbw, but it could get between bat and a pad thrust outside the line of off-stump and bowl the batsman or force him to give a catch behind the wicket on the leg-side. Conversely, a left-hander had to be wary not to edge into the slips by playing inside. Various reports comment on the trickiness of his flight. Although the word 'flight' may have been used on occasion by some reporters to mean 'line', yet the high number of times that he caught a batsman off his own bowling does suggest that his flight through the air also was deceptive and that he could make the ball dip unexpectedly. The figure for such catches is 83 out of a total of 653 catches (12.7%), which is truly remarkable especially in comparison with both statistics to-day and the number of catches he persuaded batsmen to give the wicket-keeper, a mere four higher at 87. Gunn's figures reveal a striking difference between the two bowlers with 117 catches by the wicket-keeper and only 47 by himself off his own bowling. King's flight is probably in part responsible also for some of his dismissals stumped when the batsman either ran out of his crease or was lured too far forward when playing defensively. 69 of his victims were stumped (5.7% of his total dismissals).[19] On no fewer than ten occasions he also bemused a batsman into hitting his wicket. Although he had as victims his fair share of tail-enders, it is abundantly clear that King could pose problems for leading

---

19 Gunn's percentage (8.5%) is more impressive here. That King was more likely to have a batsman stumped than be stumped himself is of little consequence since stumpings even then were less likely off fast than medium or slow bowlers.

Technique and Style

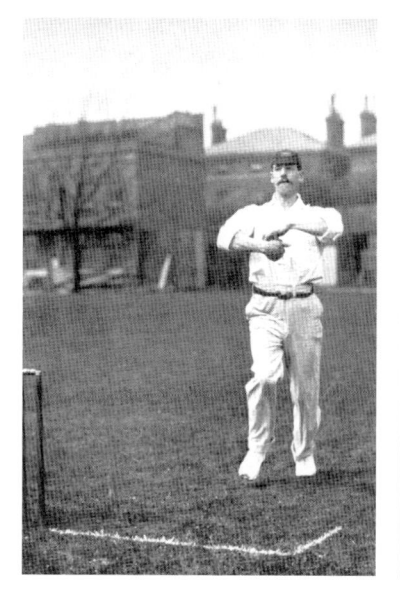

Beldam recorded King's bowling action also.

batsmen since the seven listed in Appendix One whom he dismissed ten or more times amassed 454 centuries between them in scoring 211,518 runs at a combined average of 35.87.

But King was in addition a finger-spinner getting, especially on sticky wickets, turn to the off against the right-hander, although, he did not, as Fry avers, obtain the sharp spin of a Rhodes or a Blythe. Jack Brown once said that 'with more finger-spin he would be the greatest left-hander living'. Even when, however, he merely straightened the ball rather than moved it away from the batsman, such a ball was still sufficient to hit the wickets, obtain an lbw decision or bring about a snick into the slips. The left-hander had to guard against being clean bowled, being out lbw or getting an inside edge onto the stumps or into the wicket-keeper's hands. 30.1% of his victims were bowled, 9.1% lbw and 7.2% caught by the wicket-keeper.[20] On wickets that suited him however, his spin, *pace* Fry, was by no means negligible, a South African newspaper, for instance, commenting that he 'breaks tremendously from the off' (presumably to a left-hander). One considerable advantage he had over many bowlers was his ability to be effective, at times even deadly, on slow wickets.

Although he may have done so on occasion to left-handers, I have not come across evidence that even when spinning the ball considerably on a favourable pitch he varied his direction from round to over the wicket. On this point the analytical Fry observes: 'It has often been pointed out that a bowler like Rhodes if he bowled over instead of round the wickets would obtain a sharper angle of break away from the batsman. So he would, but he would be easier to play, because the contrast between the line of the ball in the air and the direction of the break would be sacrificed.'

A prominent weapon in King's armoury as a bowler was his ability, even under punishment, to keep accurate line and especially length, the great virtues of that most economical of bowlers, Alfred Shaw. He was, therefore, fairly economical over his career, conceding an average of 43.19 runs per 100 balls, or 2.59 runs per six-ball over. Apart from the 103 five-ball overs he bowled in his first two seasons and 46 six-ball overs in his penultimate season, this average was remarkably consistent year after year whatever his average of runs per wicket: even in his very last season, when

---

20 The comparable figures for Gunn are bowled 35.0%, lbw 8.5%, caught by wicket-keeper 9.4%.

he bowled only twenty overs, this figure was 41.66. Herein he had doubtless benefited from Tom Emmett's badinage in the nets when, as Root recalls, he would chide errant bowlers with such words as 'yo couldn' bowl a houp, and until yo' can yo'll get noa time for thy bread and cheese and 'arf a pint, not if thou 'as to stop here all neeight', and the threat to bring his 'two lasses' from 'whome' to show them up. Emmett will certainly have emphasized length, and perhaps line also, to make up for his reputation as one who used to unsettle a batsman by bowling a wide immediately before the wicket-taking ball.[21] Another beneficial influence on King was, to quote Knight's words in the *Leicester Daily Mercury*, 'old Rylott, that superbly great bowler, grizzled like a prophet, but with more of a prophet's fire and fierceness, for his voice and his mien were those of a gentle woman', who retained his 'interest in bowling as a poet in his love', and passed on his knowledge of left-arm bowling both at Leicester and as chief of the ground staff at Lord's.

There are no photographs of King bowling in a match and I have found no comments on his field-placing, apart from the remark in a South African newspaper that, antecedent to his very first over in South Africa, he exercised 'the greatest care' in arranging his fielders. One must assume that for the right-hander he had very much a leg-side field with always a leg-slip and a fine leg, but a slip for the ball that he straightened,[22] and packed the mid-wicket, mid-on and mid-off regions. For the left-hander he will always have had at least one slip and packed his off-side field. He probably made no use of a very close fielder in front of the wicket except when the pitch was fiery or crumbled, since the ballooning bad-pad catches off modern, springy, light-weight pads were not created by the various types of his period. In the days when wicket-keepers would have been ashamed, or worse, to be described as glorified long-stops, King will have had his always standing up to the wickets: indeed his first county keeper, Johnny Whiteside, stood up even to their colleague Arthur Woodcock who, at least in his initial overs, did not bow the knee to even the terrifying Kortright. This practice, of course, augmented his number of victims stumped. By nature he was a combative bowler,

---

21   He once bowled 55 wides in a season, though claiming never to bowl one deliberately.
22   Did he ever on a good wicket dispense with this? Convention would have disapproved.

and on one occasion early in his career, in 1902, he even appealed, albeit unsuccessfully, for 'obstructing the field' against A.E.Relf.

His ability as a sprinter meant that, in his early days, he was an out-fielder, not infrequently in the covers, from which, with no need for the caution evident in his running between wickets as a batsman, he was a veritable Achilles in his pursuit of the ball to the boundary if it should chance to evade his long reach and athleticism. Newspapers not infrequently reported in such manner as 'he was applauded for smart work in the field'. One description of an outstanding effort may stand for others: on 3 July 1902, at Leicester, John Gunn 'hit high up over King's head at mid-off. It seemed impossible for him to get to it in time, but running hard, and swinging round at the finish to try to face the ball, he brought off a fine catch sideways.' In later days, when he had thickened a little (never very much) around the waist and his legs were slower and rheumatical, he fielded in the slips, although as late as 1923, when he was 52, he is mentioned more than once as at cover or mid-off, on one occasion as even racing back from the former to take a catch. In 1922 Knight, in reference to this phase of King's career, mentioned 'his telescopic arms and sure fingers', but he may have been envisioning him as he was in the final years before the Great War – Knight had, after all, retired from county cricket in 1912 and his duties as a school coach at Highgate School, and later at Belvedere College, Dublin, had probably prevented him from seeing much, if anything, of his friend in action after the War. *The Cricketer*, on the other hand, probably does not do him full justice in routinely contemning the county's poor post-war fielding which was apparently redeemed by no competent out-fielder or slip, for in the 157 matches King played in these years, at an age when most first-class cricketers are content to recite their exploits of yore to children or even grandchildren, he held 84 catches, a few still described as 'brilliant'.

Chapter Four
From Journeyman to Master

King's chances of a permanent career as a professional cricketer were enhanced when, in addition to being employed by his county, he joined the enormous ground staff at Lord's - that year numbering 58 - to which there already belonged the veteran Leicestershire players Rylott and John Wheeler and his team-mates Pougher, Woodcock, Whiteside and Geeson. He was to remain a member of the staff at Lord's for the rest of his playing career.[23]

It was probably in this year, 1899, that King first lodged in Lansdowne Road, Leicester, in a three-storey house owned by a Mrs York. Census returns of 1881 and 1901 show both King and his elder brother living in the parental home on Worship Street in Lutterworth, but this does not prove that during the cricket season he was not already lodging in Leicester. He retained friendly relations with his landlady's family all his life. Around this time he was also working in the off-season for Mr A.J.Lawrence in Rugby as a compositor.

King's first full season was no triumph, although in mitigation it must be remarked that he suffered at times this season from 'rheumatic gout'. In Championship matches he averaged a mere 15.17 for 349 runs, while his 17 wickets cost an expensive 43.23 each, *Wisden* commenting that he 'looked very ordinary'; and he was deservedly dropped for the last three matches of the season. As 'Reynard' was later to write, 'his talent only peeped out during his earlier years as a professional'. Nevertheless, there were sufficient encouraging signs for his county not to abandon him. He

---

23 MCC records list him on the ground staff for every season from 1899 to 1925. In the period 1899 to 1915, he played 115 one- or two-day matches for the club, scoring almost 4,500 runs at an average of just under 35. His busiest year was 1901 when he played in ten matches, some of two innings, scoring 564 runs at 35.25. He missed 1910, injured, entirely. The matches were with schools, clubs, District Associations and Minor Counties. The records are less comprehensive on his bowling returns, but he appears to have taken about 270 wickets at perhaps 15.00 or so. Sometimes captains held him back; he seemed to have bowled second-change quite often. He played in only nine matches after 1915, including one in 1917: it is possible that he umpired instead, but the scorebooks rarely give such details. In some earlier seasons where umpires' names are available, older pros often stood in the club's matches.

top-scored against the always formidable Yorkshiremen with an innings of 37 out of 112 at Bramall Lane; made 65 out of a fifth-wicket partnership of 134 with C.J.B.Wood against the 'Peakites' at Chesterfield, coming in when 'the wicket was beginning to cut up' and batting 'without blemish' despite deteriorating light; improved his best bowling analysis to four for 12 at The Oval, including bowling his future colleague, the Leicester-born V.F.S. ('Very Fast Scoring') Crawford; bowled unchanged through an innings for the first time when MCC was dismissed for 57 at Lord's (although he took only one for 27 in 21 overs while Arthur Woodcock took nine for 28); was entrusted with opening the bowling, albeit unsuccessfully, against the Australians; and made his début for MCC in first-class matches. For the first time also he had the pleasure of his brother James' company in the team against Middlesex at Lord's, although this fraternal pleasure generated no great success since between them they made but 26 runs in four innings, took a single lower-order wicket while conceding 54 runs and held no catch.

Fred Root considered King, together with others such as Rhodes, Hirst and Astill, as classic examples of players 'who have to rely almost entirely upon their bowling ability during the earlier stages of their career, later developing into recognized batsmen'. But he was surely wrong in King's case, for 1900 saw his break-through in both areas (Root was hardly right even if he was thinking solely of his sojourn at Birkenhead). After a total in his first four years of 965 runs at just over 16 an innings and 34 wickets at just over 45 each, he now, despite 'spectacles' and no wickets in the opening match against MCC, was only nine runs short of 1,000 runs for the season and his 81 wickets cost only 22.13 each, an average lower, by over 3 runs, than that for his batting, which is always the mark of a really valuable all-rounder. *Wisden* comments that he 'came out in surprising form, his advance upon anything he had previously done being most marked.... King was always attractive to the on-looker... took more wickets than anyone else, and could certainly claim to be the best all-round man on the side.'

Having never previously taken five wickets in an innings he now, on each occasion opening the bowling, performed the feat seven times, including three in consecutive innings in two matches against Worcestershire. In the first of these games he took ten wickets in a match for the first time (11 for 69), while in the two games against these opponents he had the remarkable combined figures of 17 wickets for 111 runs. His best return was seven for 91 against the champions Yorkshire, who made 302 at Huddersfield, immediately after his five for 46 had helped dismiss Nottinghamshire for 259 at home. Another notable performance was his taking of the last four Essex wickets at a personal cost of nine runs, again at Leicester, where he was unlucky to miss a hat-trick as the last man, Harry Young, 'put the ball up in dangerous proximity to Stocks at square leg'. He managed to show himself the all-rounder with a fifty and a five-wicket haul on two occasions, both away, against Worcestershire and when he and Geeson bowled unchanged in bottom county Hampshire's second innings. He also took four wickets in a match against Cambridge University, in which, for an MCC team captained by Grace, Leicestershire bowlers had a combined tally of 19 dismissals.

King began the season batting at No.7, but after scoring two fifties at The Oval he was promoted, generally to No.3. Having in his first four seasons scored only four fifties he now scored six, although only one was at home. His highest innings was 121 at Derby, excoriated by *Wisden* in carrying 'caution to excess' for taking three hours and fifty minutes but, as Lord Mancroft later observed, the English invented cricket since, 'not being a spiritual people', they needed something 'to give themselves' a 'concept of eternity' – and it was King's maiden century, made after 'a nasty smack on the finger', and not really very slow anyway.

The first year of the new century enhanced the reputation of the English climate for 'chameleon-like changes', although for the Leicestershire club it was more notable in that a move was made to a site only about a mile from the centre of the city, in the belief that greater crowds could be expected there than at the Grace Road ground which was accessible for most non-pedestrian spectators only by horse-tram. The club was right since in 1901 there were 1,500 members, as opposed to only 600 in 1897, and the following year a further 400. The creation of the new ground, nearer to the river, and of alluvium this time over the Keuper Marl, involved the levelling of a small part of the ancient earthworks, possibly part of a Roman aqueduct system, known as Raw Dykes. Prince Rupert had come this way to array his army here in 1645 for the successful siege of Leicester at which, according to local tradition, the death of the sentinel who had replaced him had brought about John Bunyan's conversion. Now the water-meadows were transformed into a pleasing ground, marred only by the gasworks to the south, although increasingly 'showers of smuts, black, sticky, and vile-tasting', in Root's words, which fell 'at almost regular intervals' were irksome to players.[24] The pitch was in the first few years very lively until by generous applications of Nottingham marl it was brought up to a higher standard. One innovation was that amateurs and professionals now entered the field through the same gate, though still from segregated dressing-rooms.

The ground was opened by the Marquis of Granby, on behalf of the Club, and the Mayor of Leicester, on behalf of the town, on 13 May, the first day of the inaugural match, against Surrey. Although Leicestershire lost, King revelled in the new surroundings to make a capital 65 in the large first innings and dominate the second with a chanceless 91 out of only 172 in 155 minutes. This performance earned him 'talent money', and 'never was it more thoroughly deserved and honestly earned than in this instance, for he faced the superb bowling of the Surrey attackers with infinite credit to himself, and at a time, too, when the majority of his colleagues seemed almost helpless against it'. He was clearly the most important man in the team this season with a batting average in Championship matches over 13 runs higher than his bowling average. Finishing second to Wood in the former and, among the regular bowlers, top in the latter discipline, he played a large rôle in Leicestershire having for the first time as many as three

When first used as Leicestershire's main ground, in 1901, Aylestone Road still had a rural aspect. King played 208 first-class matches here.

---

24 George Headley is famously reputed to have tasted the smuts in the speedily-to-be-corrected belief (or did he only mischievously pretend to such a belief?) that they were black snow.

counties below them, only one of which was actually met on the field. The side set a new record of four Championship wins and, in addition, secured victories over London County and the visiting South Africans.

King raised his highest score twice with 131 against Hampshire at Southampton in June and, 'batting correctly', 143 against Derbyshire at Glossop the next month before scoring his maiden century at Leicester in August, 135 *v* London County with 'smart off-drives at the expense of the doctor [Grace]', who opened the bowling. But he probably gained most satisfaction in the last, drawn, match of the season at The Oval when, perhaps buoyed by having Abel caught for two when 'the Guv'nor' needed 12 for a world-record seasonal aggregate, he defied the great Tom Richardson to be unbeaten with 113 out of a mere 224 after his county had lost five wickets for 44 runs. He also had the pleasure of scoring his maiden half-century for MCC in a first-class match, 50 against Worcestershire: the previous year he had scored 50 and 59 *v* Minor Counties. His selection for Mr A.J.Webbe's XI *v* Cambridge University showed the approval of his social superiors for a match in which he helped his side to victory with four for 39. Less happily he did show his susceptibility to 'lobsters', being bowled by Simpson-Hayward when well-set for 89 and then caught off him for a duck at Worcester: he was also slowed down by Jephson's 'awkward deliveries', whereas against A.J.L.Hill's lobs, after initially resisting temptation, he ran out to drive him to the boundary.

Twice also he improved his best bowling analysis, on each occasion against the 'Lacemen', as the players of Nottinghamshire were known at the time, albeit on badly rain-affected pitches. At Trent Bridge he took seven for 70 out of a total of 249, which the home players presumably considered luxury since they had been abjectly subdued by Yorkshire for only 13 in their previous match. The bowler's joy was not, however, unalloyed, for he was deprived of a hat-trick when Carlin skied the ball to mid-off only for Wood and Geeson to wait for each other as 'the ball dropped harmlessly between them'. At Leicester King took six for 22 in the first innings and then, despite poor fielding by his side, seven for 51 to give him match figures of 13 for 73, which he was never to better. Since he had dismissed four batsmen in the second innings in the other game, he had a total of twenty-four 'Lacemen' victims in the season, but what will have given him greater pleasure as a loyal team-man was that at Leicester he was not out with 24 at the finish to help his county to victory. Nevertheless of possibly even greater merit was his analysis of five for 112 in 45 overs at Scarborough when Yorkshire ran up a mammoth 562 at 3.32 runs an over.

In the notoriously wet season of 1902 Leicestershire managed to finish above four counties, including Middlesex, thanks in considerable part to King, the mainstay of the batting with Wood and Knight and of the bowling with Billy Odell. At the end of the season the local newspaper judged that he had 'worn the "running fox" with credit'. His most memorable performance came outside the Championship when he and Woodcock bowled unchanged to dismiss the Australians for 126. King himself took five for 76: besides having the captain Joe Darling and Warwick Armstrong caught, he bowled the redoubtable Victor Trumper, then in the midst of a superlative season, for 20 'with a ball that broke from the off, the batsman being too late for it'. Five weeks later, for an England XI against the same opponents, he 'batted freely' to become the second-highest scorer in the first innings before he was run out for 47, and he also had the satisfaction of bowling Monty Noble for a single in his two for 20. Although this latter match did not denote any great advance in his extra-county recognition, for the England XI was a 'moderate side' in a hastily arranged fixture and included three other Leicestershire players, his selection at last in an important match for MCC, their opening fixture against Yorkshire, did. King did not disappoint, with 46 out of a meagre total of 98 (only 89 from the bat). His best innings for Leicestershire were his two centuries, both against Worcestershire: 130 away to help his county to victory after 22 wickets had fallen on the first day; and a 'plucky' 109 not out in a losing cause at home in four and a quarter hours, when he was twice injured before he made his first run after twenty uncomfortable minutes and was later 'repeatedly struck by [G.A.] Wilson'. Not once in these two matches did he fall to Simpson-Hayward, who twice ensnared five victims.

For his county against London County, he took the wicket of W.G.Grace for the first time of three in consecutive seasons.[25] After inducing him to snick a ball just over his stumps King had him caught for eight very low down by Geeson at first slip, 'one of the best catches ever seen at the Palace . . . W.G. did not like the

---

25   Leicestershire did not play Gloucestershire until 1919.

decision but had to go'. In the MCC match against the same opponents, he appeared together with the creator of Sherlock Holmes, Sir Arthur Conan Doyle, whom he had met the year before in the opposition. King himself scored 37 and 53, but C.J.B.Wood, in scoring 176 for London County, showed that he was fully cognisant with all his county colleague's wiles as a bowler.

The weather in 1903 was bad with 'Scotch mists' and 'continuous downpour'. Even on one of the better days in May the local newspaper pronounced: 'As in the olden days when there was much rejoicing at the return of the prodigal one, there was much pleasure in the hearts of cricketers when it was discovered that the clerk of the weather had come, in some degree, to a proper sense of his May duties. Old Sol's winter sleep, behind leaden clouds, which seemed to hold an unlimited supply of rain, appeared, however, to have done very little good in the way of giving him strength.' King retained his importance to Leicestershire in 1903, being second among both the batsmen and the regular bowlers (to Knight and Gill respectively) with his batting average again being the higher, albeit by under three runs. His failure to obtain 50 Championship wickets on pitches often unfavourable to batting - only occasionally was he entrusted this season with the new ball -

The Leicestershire side of 1903, at the back of the Aylestone Road pavilion. Standing (l to r): T.Emmett (coach), James King (J.H.'s brother), A.E.Knight, H.Whitehead, J.H.King, G.C.Gill and T.Burdett (Honorary Secretary). Seated: F.W.Stocks, W.W.Odell, V.F.S.Crawford, A.E.Davis (wk) and C.J.B.Wood. Kneeling: T.C.Allsopp and S.Coe. The appointed captain, C.E.de Trafford, is absent.

Leicestershire's scorebook, showing King's hat-trick against Sussex at Hove in July 1903.

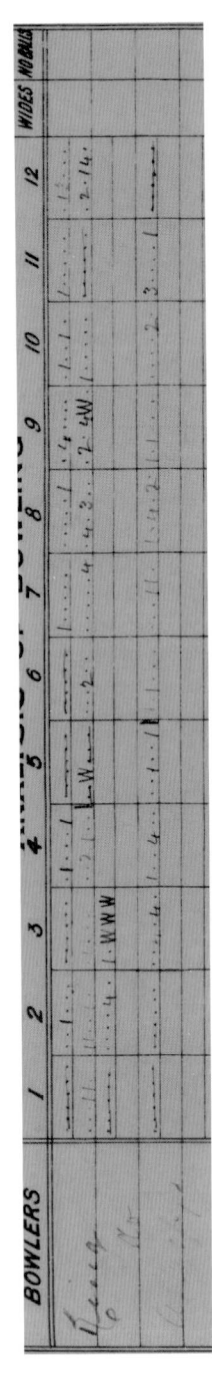

contributed greatly to his county's unexpectedly miserable record and the sharing of bottom place with Hampshire, so much had his colleagues come to rely on him. There were, nevertheless, a few bright spots. He increased his top score to 167 with a brilliant innings in four and a quarter hours against Derbyshire in which he gave only a single chance, in the deep upon reaching his century: and he twice cut Bestwick to the boundary the very next ball after being hit by him. An innings of 40 runs fewer and half an hour more against the 'Lacemen' at Trent Bridge was even more to be admired. With a score of 739 for seven, the home team acquired a first-innings lead of 508: Leicestershire followed on, but King, who very unusually had opened, and Knight then put on 241, a county record at the time for the second wicket. 'Bowling changes, silly balls, good balls, tempting balls, were all unavailing, the two "K's" treated them all with courtesy'; and Leicestershire in the end comfortably saved the game with eight wickets still to fall; it was perhaps after this stand that the screen-shifters presented him with a now lost commemorative miniature bat.

In bowling he only once took five Championship wickets in an innings, five for 57, helped by his county's first hat-trick in first-class cricket – H.T. Arnall-Thompson and A.D.Pougher had performed the feat prior to 1894 against Yorkshire and MCC respectively – when he took the last three Sussex wickets at Hove, Cox caught by the ''keeper running back', Butt 'smartly stumped' and Bland caught at cover. But his outstanding performance was a 'wonderful piece of bowling' (*Wisden*), again against Sussex, for MCC when he took five for only 6 runs to end the innings. A curious feature of the Philadelphians' match at Leicester was that both teams opened their bowling, successfully, with a King, J.B. taking seven wickets and J.H. five.

Very early in the following season, on 22 May, his father died at the age of 85 from gangrene. His doctor wished to amputate a leg, but the old builder asseverated that he preferred to die with his leg on than live without it. James Temple King left an estate of £4,540 11s 9d, one house ('Fashoda'), five cottages, one coach-house, seven villas, land and stables; and he lived long enough to be proud of his youngest son's accomplishments on the cricket field.

Leicestershire exceeded expectations, finishing equal seventh with Warwickshire and winning nine matches in all, including six in the Championship. Performances in the first half of the season were superlative and excited Knight to rhetorical ecstasy: 'I have no desire to unwind the golden threads or to jingle the silver bells, for the gratifying successes of the county are far too eloquent for any analysis, and analysis of eloquence is too much akin to a dissection of the body, and implies the death of its subject . . . we no longer halt and stumble over the rough fields, but whirl along as swiftly and successfully as a dancer whirling o'er a well waxed floor'.

King, fourth in both batting and bowling averages, was not, however, as dominant as usual, the latter average being high at 29.14 and the former enormously boosted by non-Championship matches. Nevertheless there were still some notable performances. Once more he raised his highest score, this time to 186 at Southampton, one of his favourite grounds, hitting 27 fours, mainly with 'masterly drives', and giving but a single hard chance at 158; but Hampshire was a poor team (losing by an innings and 219 runs and finishing bottom of the Championship that year) and Leicestershire made merry at over 100 runs an hour in their innings, although 'at times the ball wanted a lot of watching'. At home against Worcestershire the county was left to make 350 to win in the fourth innings, a feat never before accomplished, but won by five wickets. *Wisden* called it 'one of the biggest things ever done in the County Championship', all the more meritorious since, according to the reporter of the *Leicester Daily Mercury*, 'the pitch was in a dangerous condition'. King's stand with Coe was 'probably the pluckiest ever seen in Leicester', and the match 'one of the most sensational . . . it has been my portion to witness'. King, the mainstay, remained undefeated with

117 runs to his name in 225 minutes with 13 fours and was further rewarded by a collection of £6 11s 0d (Coe and Whitehead receiving £3 3s 0d each). In helping Leicestershire crush MCC at Lord's by an innings and 153 runs, Knight (203) and King (128), on a much easier wicket, put on 291 for the third wicket, a county record until 1961. As to bowling, King performed superbly at Edgbaston to take seven for 55 and five for 64, the wicket being very bad for only the first Warwickshire innings. Against London County he achieved his statistically best-ever analysis in a second innings with seven for 32 and dismissed his future colleague J.J.Kotze twice, although the latter returned the favour when the South Africans visited Leicester.

King was chosen for his only North *v* South game this year (curiously Knight had played for 'Players of the South' *v* 'Gentleman of England' the previous year). He justified his selection with 92, 'hitting very cleanly and with excellent judgment'; and produced a watchful innings of the same score also for MCC against Derbyshire. In addition he took six wickets in the two innings and scored 44 and 60 for Mr G.J.V.Weigall's XI *v* Cambridge University, and showed the right spirit for the occasion by getting stumped for six in the first of his five appearances at the Scarborough Festival. But it was another representative match that was destined to make his name resound throughout the cricketing world.

Chapter Five
The Match of the Season

In years when there was no touring team from Australia the match of the season was, as it had been in pre-Test times, the annual encounter between the Gentlemen and Players at Lord's. Indeed, so popular had it become that additional matches were sometimes scheduled at The Oval, Prince's, Hove, Scarborough and Hastings. Since in 1904 there were no Australians, the match had no rival for the cricketing social occasion of the year. Two fine teams had been selected, and on the morning of Monday, 4 July, grooms were adorning their well-curried horses, butlers were packing hampers with choice foods and wines, ladies and gentlemen were putting the finishing touches to their toilettes.

Then a sudden crisis arose: Johnny Tyldesley, who three days before in scoring 225 on a beautiful wicket at Trent Bridge had been hit severely in the ribs, decided that he was unfit to play. King, who was still on the MCC staff and, because Leicestershire had no match, at Lord's that morning, was chosen to take his place. He had been in fairly good form so far that season, but serendipity enabled him to take part in the match that brought him immediate fame and for which, over a hundred years later, he is still best remembered.

The match lived up to anticipation: *Wisden* described it as 'emphatically the match of the season', being 'played through from the first ball to the last in the keenest and most sportsmanlike way' and ending 'amid intense excitement late on the third afternoon'. It was, moreover, enjoyed by a huge crowd, undoubtedly the largest of King's career so far, with no fewer than 33,202 spectators paying for admission over the three days.

'From some cause', reports *Wisden*, 'probably owing to a little damp remaining in the ground, the ball . . . kicked up in a way that recalled to old habitués the cricket that used to be seen at Lord's in the sixties.' Despite valiant resistance from Tom Hayward on a bumpy pitch Hesketh Hesketh-Prichard, enjoying the most prolific season of his career, and first-change Bernard Bosanquet swiftly

The Match of the Season

reduced the Players to 62 for four and then 113 for five when King came to the wicket. In only 75 minutes he added 88 runs to the score with the Surrey man and then a further 83 with Rhodes. When he was finally seventh out, caught off Gilbert Jessop, he had batted somewhat over two and a half hours for a personal score of 104 out of 171. He had hit 14 fours and 'batted with perfect confidence all through his innings, getting most of his runs by splendid off driving'.

King was not called upon to perform with the ball, not even in the Gentlemen's second innings – the Players had a strong bowling side and, as a replacement for Tyldesley, he was obviously being played as a batsman. Leonard Braund was largely responsible for the dismissal of the Gentlemen for a mere 171 and a deficit of 156 by three o'clock on the Tuesday afternoon. But the wicket was now at its worst and Hesketh-Prichard's bowling 'quite dangerous'. After an opening stand of 35, three wickets fell at 42, and at 49 King's county colleague Knight, selected after his century the previous year, was struck on the left hand by Hesketh-Prichard, breaking a bone that kept him out of cricket for the next month. A.A.Thomson opines that the Hampshire bowler, a doughty hunter renowned for his moose-calling and a valorous soldier, 'can hardly have done more skilful sniping during the war'. King, however, outdid even his magnificent first innings as he shepherded the tail to save his side. At close of play the total was 247 for eight, but J.T.Hearne could not stay with his partner the next morning and was out with only eight runs added, with King taking 'out his bat for 109 – a wonderful display on such a wicket', according to *Wisden*, and one whose value was highlighted by the fact that nobody else could contribute more than Rhodes, who managed a mere 31. King's two-fold performance enabled him to equal the achievement of the amateur R.E.Foster, who had in 1900 also scored two centuries in this famous encounter: they were not joined in this select group until Duleepsinhji's efforts in 1930, and in the whole history of these matches, at Lord's, the Oval, Prince's, Hove, Folkestone, Hastings and Scarborough, no other player achieved the feat, King being, then, left alone to uphold the professionals' banner. The wicket, however, had rolled out in a way that surprised everyone; but, despite the fact that the Gentlemen managed to achieve a most unexpected victory with splendid and aggressive batting, the match became known as 'King's Match' and the telegrams and letters poured in. The *Manchester Guardian* proclaimed his performance as one 'which has eclipsed everything

The Match of the Season

Lord's Ground.

GENTLEMEN v. PLAYERS.

MONDAY, TUESDAY & WEDNESDAY, JULY 4, 5, 6, 1904.

PLAYERS.	First Innings.		Second Innings.	
1 Hayward	st Payne, b Bosanquet	88	c Payne, b Prichard	14
2 Iremonger	run out	10	c Foster, b Prichard	24
3 Denton	c Jessop, b Prichard	4	b Prichard	0
4 Knight	c Foster, b Prichard	7	retired hurt	2
5 Braund	c Foster, b Prichard	0	c Bosanquet, b Jackson	2
6 J. Gunn	l b w, b Bosanquet	22	st Payne, b Bosanquet	17
7 King	c McDonell, b Jessop	104	not out	109
8 Rhodes	c Payne, b Bosanquet	50	b Jackson	31
9 Arnold	b Jessop	8	c Bosanquet, b Prichard	14
10 Lilley (Capt.)	c Payne, b Jackson	4	b Jones	17
11 J. T. Hearne	not out	0	c Jackson, b Prichard	2
	B 12, l-b 3, w 3, n-b ,	24	B 19, l-b 3, w , n-b 1,	23
	Total	327	Total	255

FALL OF THE WICKETS.
1-33 2-48 3-56 4-62 5-113 6-201 7-284 8-293 9-325 10-327
1-35 2-42 3-42 4-42 5-31 6-164 7-193 8-247 9-255 10-

ANALYSIS OF BOWLING. 1st Innings.   2nd Innings.
Name.   O.   M.   R.   W. Wd. N-b.   O.   M.   R.   W. Wd. N-b.
McDonell   21   5   58   0   2   ...
Prichard   39   12   102 3   24   4   80   5   ... ...
Bosanquet   17   1   78   3   10   0   46   1   ... ...
Jackson   15.5 4   31   1   1   ...   24   5   67   2   ... ...
Jessop   10   0   34   2   5   0   31   0   ... 1
Jones   2   0   8   1   ... ...

GENTLEMEN.	First Innings.		Second Innings.	
1 H. K. Foster, Esq.	b Arnold	0	c Lilley, b Hearne	52
2 R. H. Spooner, Esq.	run out	23	c and b Braund	6
3 C. B. Fry, Esq.	b Braund	32	c and b Hearne	41
4 K. S. Ranjitsinhji	b Braund	5	c Lilley, b Arnold	121
5 Hon. F. S. Jackson (Capt.)	b Braund	53	c Lilley, b Arnold	80
6 A. O. Jones, Esq.	c Lilley, b Braund	4	not out	56
7 G. L. Jessop, Esq.	st Lilley, b Braund	12	c Denton, b Hearne	2
8 B. J. T. Bosanquet, Esq.	c Lilley, b Arnold	9	c Lilley, b Arnold	22
9 M. W. Payne, Esq.	c Lilley, b Arnold	1	run out	10
10 H. C. McDonell, Esq.	b Braund	1		
11 Hesketh Prichard, Esq.	not out	10	not out	4
	B 15, l-b 1, w , n-b ,	16	B 14, l-b 1, w 1, n-b 2,	18
	Total	171	Total	412

FALL OF THE WICKETS.
1-4 2-46 3-60 4-60 5-70 6-90 7-107 8-111 9-112 10-171
1-85 2-100 3-108 4-302 5-315 6-320 7-375 8-400 9- 10-

ANALYSIS OF BOWLING. 1st Innings.   2nd Innings.
Name.   O.   M.   R.   W. Wd. N-b.   O.   M.   R.   W. Wd. N-b.
Hearne   10   1   32   0   37   10   97   3   ... ...
Arnold   24   6   65   3   ... ...   31.3 5   123 3   1   2
Braund   20.5 6   50   6   30   4   165 1   ... ...
Rhodes   3   0   8   0   13   3   32   0   ... ...
Gunn   12   0   37   0   ... ...

Umpires—Titchmarsh and Phillips.   Scorers—Burton and Martin.

GENTLEMEN WON BY 2 WICKETS.

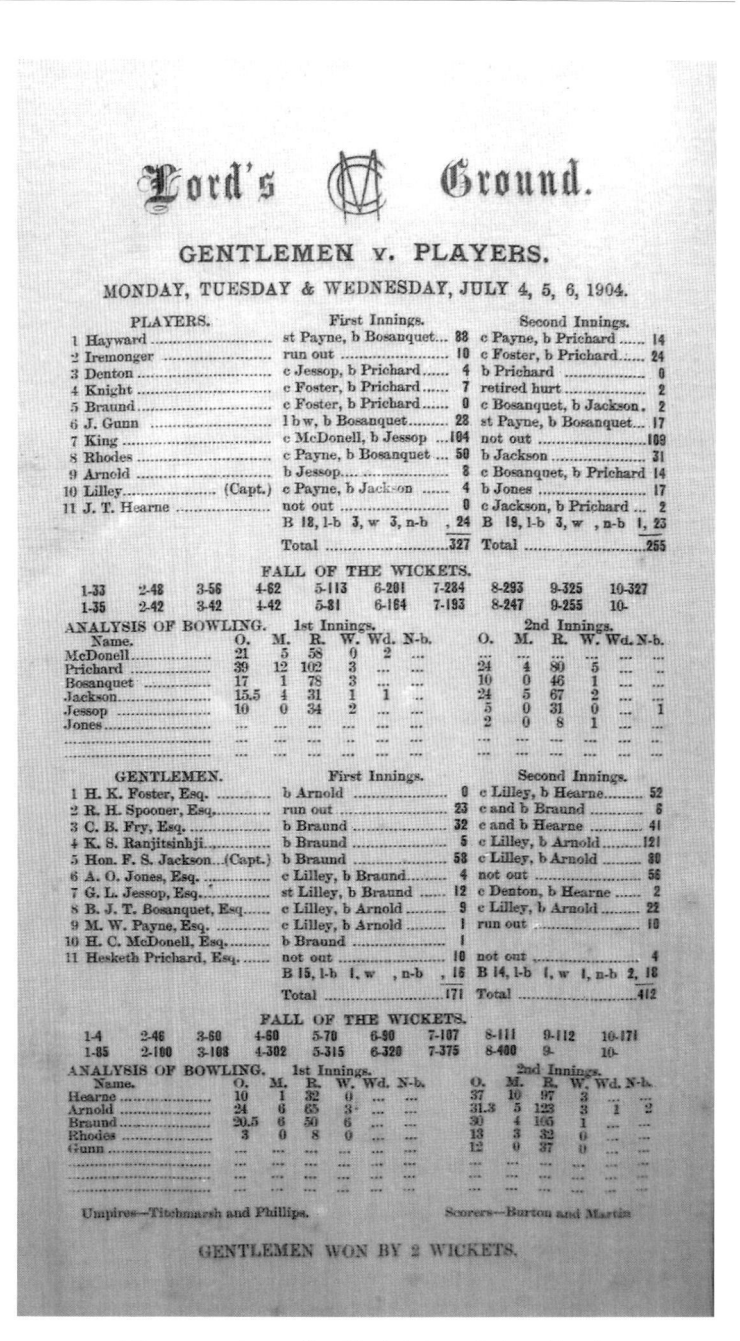

Silk scorecard recording King's twin centuries at Lord's.

he has ever done before, and has promoted him at a stroke to the first rank of batting fame', while the *Morning Leader* asserted that 'King has enrolled himself among the immortals'.

Close-up of the mellowing, narrow-grained Gunn and Moore bat used by King to score two famous centuries for the Players at Lord's in 1904.

There was a 'colonial' team touring England that year – the South Africans. Although they were very successful, winning ten and losing only two of their 22 first-class matches, they had been awarded no Test. Instead a match had been arranged at Lord's a week after the conclusion of Gentlemen *v* Players against 'An England XI'. This was clearly not an English first team, and it lost by 189 runs: its only 'redeeming feature' was the batting of King who, mastering Kotze on this occasion, top-scored in both innings with 55 out of 167 and 72 out of 203. Only one other player reached the thirties in either innings, and King had the satisfaction of scoring more runs than the great 'Ranji'. This time his bowling was also used, and all told he took four wickets for 91, twice dismissing Maitland Hathorn, the No.3 and highest scorer in the South African second innings.

Perhaps surprisingly King was not considered for the Players at Lord's the following year: he played instead for Leicestershire against Sussex. But he was chosen for The Oval match against a weak Gentlemen's team, in which he was joined by three county colleagues. These were C.J.B.Wood, who opened for the Gentlemen, Knight, who scored over a hundred runs in all, and Billy Odell, who took ten wickets. King himself performed reasonably with 19 and 39, being bowled in both innings by the George Beldam to whose photographs we are indebted for evidence of King's bowling style and off-drive.

It is often forgotten that in 1906 King gave performances almost rivalling those of two years earlier; but this time the match was at The Oval. He did not score a century and all eyes were on W.G.Grace who made 74, at the venerable age of 58, in the second innings before being out to King's colleague, Tom Jayes. As a batsman King had to face, among others, Gilbert Jessop, J.N.Crawford and Odell, against all of whom he was top-scorer in the first innings with an undefeated 89. In the second, after his team had lost five wickets for a mere handful of runs, he made 88 in a partnership of 182 with Joe Hardstaff. Then, when he was well set on the third day, 'W.G. went on and with his first ball seduced King into attempting a big hit, only to send the ball into the hands of long-on'. In after years King may have taken some consolation for his failure to make a third hundred in these games from the realisation that he was the very last victim in first-class cricket of the round-arm arch-deceiver.[26] He also, this time, did bowl himself, having Jessop caught for a duck in his two for 37.

King's final appearances for the Players were in 1909, when he made a mere 8 and 12 not out at Lord's and at Scarborough where in a match ruined by rain he was out for nought but had Johnny Douglas caught by Jack Hobbs. In total his figures in these Gentlemen *v* Players matches were 468 runs with two centuries and two fifties at an average of 78.00, three wickets for 68 runs and two catches.

---

26   King was caught by L.G.Colbeck, who had won his second Blue for Cambridge University a fortnight before: he played occasionally for Middlesex.

Chapter Six
Successes and Disappointments

King's triumph in the Gentlemen *v* Players' match led to his appointment as professional with the Western Province Club in Cape Town, South Africa, for the following winter. He was not the first Leicestershire cricketer to coach abroad. In 1893 Arthur Woodcock had been employed by Haverford College near Philadelphia, where in his honest and laconic manner he praised good points and rapidly spotted bad to produce competent players out of mediocre and transform J.A.Lester from a batsman of no achievements to one averaging over 100 in his first season. 'Woody', as he was known there, was considered the best coach ever to be appointed by the school; but, unlike King's, his duties did not include playing.

Although the matches did not have first-class status, the standard was assuredly not mean. Among King's colleagues were three Test players: Johannes Jacobus Kotze, who toured England three times, had played for London County the previous summer and was considered the fastest bowler ever to appear in South Africa; H.M.Taberer, who had played two seasons in England for Oxford University; and Murray Bisset, later knighted, who had captained South Africa in two Tests in 1898/99 and led the touring party to England in 1901, and who ended his days as acting Governor of Rhodesia. Allan Reid and Murray Bisset's brother Arthur had been members of the touring party in 1901. Although Western Province C.C. had the strongest team in the Senior Championship, Cape Town could boast the Test players S.D. and S.J.Snooke: the other clubs were Alma, Claremont, Diocesan College, Green Point and South Africa College.

At King's début for his new team, at No.3 in a home match against Alma, he 'was given a hearty and encouraging cheer on proceeding to the wickets', according to a local reporter who reminded his readers that King 'was one of the most consistent of our English batsmen . . . and secured the great distinction in either innings for the Players. It was, therefore, not surprising to see a capital gate at

*The Western Province club side in 1904/05.
Standing (l to r): H.W.Carolin, Capt Wadlow, W.A.Hicks, R.Buchanan, J.H.King, A.V.C.Bissett and Gnr Smith (umpire).
Seated: P.S.T.Jones, A.Reid, M.Bisset (capt), F.B.Moore and J.J.Kotze.
On the ground: H.M.Taberer and A.N.Difford.
Six of King's colleagues played first-class cricket.*

Newlands, the majority of those present probably coming chiefly to watch the initial performance of King for the Province.' King did not disappoint, although the reporter adds that 'the well-known maxim that the King can do no wrong was not altogether borne out, as when his total had reached 37, made up mostly by strong straight drives and neat leg glances, a beauty from the inimitable Rain . . . got clean past his defence'. Given the honour of opening the bowling (Kotze was not playing) he and H.W.Carolin then took five wickets each, bowling unchanged through Alma's innings of 92 to give their team a lead of 110. King's overall statistics for the season, in which Western Province won the Senior Championship, I have unfortunately not been able to ascertain.

For the winter of 1905/06 King returned to South Africa. Western Province had clearly found King not only a very able performer but also a good 'team-man'. One reporter observed of an innings that 'the "pro" was playing the proper game; no thoughts of average disturbed him in the pursuit of runs'. Nonetheless his club cannot have found fault with his averages that season, which make fine reading. Batting: innings 18, not out 2, runs 697, highest score 106, average 43.56. Bowling: overs 184.5, maidens 45, runs 513, wickets 35, average 14.65. His average for batting was, therefore, only a fraction under three times that for bowling, a statistic reminiscent of Grace in his best years. For his club King topped the batting averages and aggregates, and the fact that he was only third in the bowling averages (and fourth in number of wickets) with so low a figure is a striking indication of his batting mastery. After giving such sterling service he must have been disappointed not to have his employment extended, a decision taken for a solely economic reason, as the *South African Annual* in its review of the season 1905/06 for the Western Province club makes quite clear: 'J.H.King was again engaged as professional and proved very useful both in batting and bowling, whilst his duties were carried out in the same obliging and courteous manner as during the previous season. The committee, having carefully considered the matter, recommended that no steps be taken to get a professional from England for the next season. . . . It is with great reluctance that the committee have come to this decision, but they feel the necessity for reducing expenditure is imperative.'

In 1905 Leicestershire attained fifth position in the Championship, its highest until it came third in 1953, long after King's death, and he was never again to figure in a team finishing in the top half of the competition. Surprisingly, however, this achievement owed little to the all-rounder. *Wisden* commented on his decline in both disciplines, perhaps a little unfairly since in Championship matches his batting average was still one above that for bowling and the latter was superior to his corresponding figure in 1904; but he took only 33 wickets in the Championship.

After a promising start with 69 and 50 against Warwickshire in the second match of the season he suffered an injury to a hand in the following match against Yorkshire, missed the following three fixtures and perhaps returned too early – the *Leicester Daily Mercury* certainly attributed his poor season to this injury. He achieved nothing of note until early July with five for 39 in the second innings against a woeful Derbyshire, sixteen of whose batsmen were bowled out, an extraordinary quantity for the twentieth century; and 95 and 43* *v* Sussex. Confidence in his batting was not restored by opening at Northampton in early August, although he achieved the rare double of opening both batting and bowling, a thing that Alan Shipman regularly did in later years for Leicestershire. In the penultimate match, however, he had the satisfaction of bundling Lancashire out for 222 after MacLaren and Spooner had scored a swift 102, dismissing both openers and three of the next six batsmen to finish with five for 58 and give his side a lead of 64.

Before his woes began he had been largely responsible for a win by MCC against Nottinghamshire, being equal top scorer with 37, and taking four for 26 to finish off an easy victory in a substantially rain-damaged match. At the wrong time of the season for him, he was also selected in 'a very powerful side to meet the Australians' (*Wisden*), in which he batted as low as No.8, but most of the game was lost to rain.

The final Championship match of the season, against Surrey at The Oval, was the last in which elder brother James appeared for his county. He never made the grade, scoring but 83 runs at 10.38 with a highest score of 24 not out and taking two wickets for 146 runs in seven matches spread over the years 1899 to 1905; although he did end his career with a defiant and unbeaten 18 after his brother had top-scored with 57. His most important contribution to the county side was probably the original scoring system that he instituted in the nets. In addition to an engagement with Sefton Park, he was a stalwart member of the Leicester Town Club (known at its foundation in 1866 as the Victoria Park club and from 1878 as the Leicester Cricket Club). For 36 years he was the much-loved licensee of the Avenue Hotel on Cavendish Road in Aylestone Park not far from the Grace Road ground, and he assisted his successor for about ten years thereafter. Although he appeared 'solemn' to the youthful Philip Snow, his niece always remembered his unfailing cheerfulness and kindness: 'He was a lovely person. Despite a terrible life he was never downcast [and] was very fond of poets, particularly Burns and Byron. [He] used to walk at night with terriers Vicky and Tinker and a tabby tom-cat.' On one occasion he made his way to Knighton and 'stood under the bridge' for better acoustics as he recited from *Childe Harold's Pilgrimage*. When he reached the words 'There was a sound of revelry by night' (3.21.1), he was disturbed by the applause of a policeman who had tarried to listen. He died nearly sixteen months after his brother, and they are buried together.

1906 was a most disappointing season, one critic opining that Leicestershire was 'a litter of pink-eyed rabbits, and if animals of that breed walk up to be shot, the phrase is an apt one'. The county finished fifteenth, albeit with three victories, a result generally of poor team spirit and the inability of bowlers to bowl well on good wickets. King, though obtaining over 1,000 runs, managed to reach

Successes and Disappointments

50 only six times in 49 innings, and he again took only 33 Championship wickets, his average for the former discipline being now far lower than for the latter. Maybe his exertions in South Africa were taking their toll. His best return was four for 23 to conclude victory over Worcestershire. In batting he made 126* at Glossop against the bottom-place club, and 118 in an eventually successful attempt to save the last home match of the season, against Warwickshire, but there is something worrying about being stumped in such a situation. Going in at No.3 against Essex he carried his bat unavailingly for 54, but the fact that he scored only about a quarter of the runs while he was at the wicket suggests an innings of great determination (an inheritance from Robert the Bruce?) rather than fluency and confidence.

There was one curious incident in the match at The Oval: 'King played a ball down against his stumps, chopped it out, moved a yard forward, and more in fun than anything else, called Knight' for a run. Upon a half-hearted appeal from Tom Hayward and after a full minute's consultation between the umpires W.A.J.West and A.Millward, he was given out 'hit the ball twice', the eighth time in the history of first-class cricket that a batsman had been thus dismissed. There was no further instance for just over fifty years, although it later became quite popular in the 1980s in the sub-continent; it is still the most recent instance in England. It is perhaps fitting that this 'distinction' should go to a Leicestershire player, since it was in a match between players of Leicester and Coventry in 1788 that there arose about this very issue a dispute which was 'submitted to the first reputed cricket society in the Kingdom',[27] the earliest recorded instance of MCC being asked to adjudicate over a legal matter. King's dismissal was, however, moot and the subject of much controversy since Law 27 at the time stated simply: 'The striker is out . . . if the ball be struck, or be stopped by any part of his person, and he willfully strike it again, except that it be done for the purpose of guarding his wicket, which he may do with his bat, or any part of his person, except his hands . . . ': there is no mention of subsequent running.

Leicestershire began the new campaign in 1907 disastrously, losing the first five matches, but gradually the new captain, Sir Arthur Hazlerigg (later the first Baron) of Noseley Hall, instilled a new spirit in the team, which began to win matches by mid-July to

---

27   Unattributed quotation in John Major, *More than a Game: the Story of Cricket's Early Years*, p 109.

finish a creditable eleventh with six victories. It is perhaps significant that all of King's better performances came in the August, but he had a very poor year by his standards, with an average of only 18.08 for batting in which he never really came to grips with the generally poor conditions. On occasions he batted as low as No.7. He did have an excuse: after opening the season for MCC he missed his county's first three games because of an injury to a finger and perhaps returned too early. He came back for an exciting tied game against MCC, in which he did score a crucial second innings of 51, but then found it hard to score consistently. Past performances, however, kept him in the home crowd's favour, and he received 'a sympathetic cheer as he scored his first run' against Derbyshire after four consecutive ducks in early August. His best innings, in August, was one of 80* in which he played 'with great skill and judgment' (*Wisden*) in helping to save the game against Hampshire. Although he bowled little, his average in this sphere was an excellent 17.63, with a best analysis of four for 33 *v* Derbyshire (combined with an innings of 57), while in the final game of the season he had match figures of six for 97 at The Oval. One landmark was that on 4 July he opened the bowling for the first time with one who was to become his partner on many successful occasions, Ewart Astill.

Upon the conclusion of the season, on 25 September, King was married at St Andrew's, Aylestone, a church best known for its huge fourteenth-century chancel – perhaps the largest of any village church – and for its record of the wedding of Dorothy Vernon to John Manners which disproves the romantic tale of an

Bouquets, millinery and red bricks.
Guests at King's wedding reception in September 1907.
A.E.Knight is third from the right in the middle row.

elopement from Haddon Hall. King's bride, following an engagement of eight years, was Florence Norton, the daughter of a mill-furnisher. She was 30, he 36. It was a very happy marriage and they had one daughter, Margaret Bruce, born on 15 February 1909.

Florence was a remarkable woman in her own right. Their daughter remembered her keeping fit by riding a penny-farthing bicycle and walking on stilts in the garden, two activities surely likely to have sown amazement if not consternation amongst their neighbours, and the former of which curiously brings to mind the fact that the old County Ground, on which her husband made his début for Leicestershire, had been the scene of a 'Fifty Miles Championship' race for penny-farthing cyclists in 1887. Nonetheless, she did not have the nerve to watch her husband bat for fear of seeing him hurt, preferring to 'watch for him at home' where she 'would open the door and step out to meet him at the front gate as he got off the tram'. She ruled the household, he the garden, which 'was huge, and he did everything' himself. Margaret did, nevertheless, remember her father at home as 'an excellent chef' for the game and fish that he shot and caught himself. He had, however, to keep his shooting dogs with a friend, Arthur Brown,

Florence King with daughter Margaret.

John and Florence King and their daughter Margaret in the garden of their house on Aylestone Road.

'because mother would not have them in the house'. King was devoted to her, and when she died at the early age of 53 he was quite bereft emotionally and 'never the same again'.

For the first few years the newly wedded couple lived in some rooms in 'Shelbrooke', the home that King's new father-in-law had built in the late nineteenth century onto the pre-existing 551 Aylestone Road ('Rutland House') to form a semi-detached pair. This was almost opposite Duncan Road, which led to the southern entrance to the old Grace Road ground where King had begun his first-class career. It was also only about a mile's walk from the new ground further north on the same road. The house had a large garden behind and a paddock adjacent to the Grand Union Canal, with the River Soar beyond. The area was more rural then than now, daughter Margaret learning to swim in the canal and kingfishers nesting in the bank below the arbour shown in the familial photograph.

Married life perhaps helped King return to normal productivity on the cricket field the following season, 1908, in which he batted consistently, reaching fifty on twelve occasions, and increased his haul of wickets to 74, although only 51 of these were in the Championship. More significantly for the history of English cricket King was not alone in making a new beginning, for the Leicestershire committee scheduled the first match of the season (against Warwickshire) to commence on a Saturday, thus giving a trial to what was to prove of enormous financial benefit to all the counties in the Championship for many years until the recent chaotic programming consequent upon first-class cricket's relegation to second-class status.[28] The county celebrated with a victory, and King with a second-innings 55 and a five-wicket haul that included the final dismissal of the match, a decisive 'Field b King 0'.

His best innings was at Northampton where, on a pitch of considerable difficulty, he and Sam Coe proceeded to add 249 for the fourth wicket against the hapless 'Cobblers' in three and a

---

28   With regard to this innovation Eric Snow vaticinally mused in 1949 on whether 'what Leicestershire cricket thinks to-day, English cricket thinks to-morrow', to be proved a successful seer when in 1962 Mike Turner introduced the 'Midlands Knock-out Competition' (in which each county was limited to one innings consisting of a maximum of 65 overs), the immediate forerunner of the following season's 'Gillette Cup Competition' and thus of all the modern cricket that is limited in overs and variety. Leicestershire celebrated the inauguration of this initial competition with a victory over Derbyshire, though subsequently losing the final to Northamptonshire.

quarter hours. King's 142 was faultless and included 19 fours. After a fairly quiet start he 'opened out in really brilliant fashion', mainly from vigorous driving interspersed with cuts and skilful leg-side strokes. In bowling he began the season in fine form against Warwickshire as we have seen, and ended it with six- and five-wicket hauls against Kent and Surrey respectively. His outstanding performance of the season, however, was for MCC, for whom he scored 60 when opening the innings and was by far the most successful bowler in taking seven for 77 and five for 133 in the Lord's match against Cambridge University. Oddly, *Wisden* did not think fit to mention his marathon bowling analyses (75.4 overs in all) in its 220-word summary. For the very last match of the season, while his colleagues Knight and Astill were playing for an England XI on Broadhalfpenny Down against a Fry-led Hambledon, King was chosen for Mr J.Bamford's XI to give practice at the Oldfields Ground, Uttoxeter, to the MCC tourists in Australia the coming winter. He managed that with a fine 60* out of 180 in the first innings and had the satisfaction of catching Jack Hobbs off his own bowling for his only wicket. His county was clearly satisfied with his performances, for of the £50 awarded by the committee as 'talent money' King received the lion's share of £9 5s 0d.

'Reynard', summing up Leicestershire's summer of 1909 in the local paper, wrote of 'another melancholy season', even a 'decedence from their [previous] mediocre standard', 'inconsistence [being] the snake in the root of [their] cricket'. King was 'the stay of the side' with batting and bowling figures similar to those of the previous year, but, though the only batsman to average over thirty for his county, he scored no century, the highest of his eleven fifties being 90 on an easy wicket at The Oval in the final match. More meritorious was his 59 against the same opponents at home which came near to saving the match, and 36 on a treacherous wicket at Northampton, where the only other batsmen to reach double figures in the last innings, after all hope had been abandoned at King's fall, were Nos.10 and 11. Despite taking 55 economical Championship wickets, he had five in an innings only twice. Outside the championship he scored 56 against the Australians in the massive total of 567 by an England XI which contained four of his county colleagues. Knight scored a magnificent 163 with but a single chance, but King's greatest distinction this season came in a match still to be described.

Chapter Seven
The Test-Match Player

'Please be Lords Monday to play England if chosen Leveson Gower County Ground Bournemouth.' Thus ran a telegram to King dated 11 July 1909.

Perhaps never in the history of cricket, at least before the 'd'Oliveira affair', has so much wrath been incurred by Test selectors as in 1909. The announcement of the fourteen players from whom the team would be chosen on the morning of the Lord's Test against the Australians ignited a conflagration that attracted far more fire-raisers than fire-fighters.

The selection committee for 1909 was Lord Hawke as chairman, C.B.Fry and H.D.G.Leveson Gower. When F.S.Jackson had declined the captaincy, A.C.MacLaren was appointed in his stead for the series. Even before the commencement of the First Test Hawke had retired to Aix-les-Bains for reason of health; while Fry, having taken part in the selection of the party, was not involved in the choice of the final eleven, or in the match as a player, since he was appearing in a long drawn-out case at the Temple where he revelled in exchanging courtesies with the distinguished counsel Sir Rufus Isaacs. In his autobiography Fry admits, 'I did not like the team when we chose it', but he prided himself on having 'rather forced' his fellow county colleague Albert Relf, England's only successful bowler, on the other members.

There were two enforced changes for Lord's from the team at Edgbaston: Fry was unavailable and Colin Blythe's nervous disposition, not for the only time, rendered him, on the advice of a specialist, unfit to be considered. In addition Gilbert Jessop – 'indispensable' according to *Wisden* – Wilfred Rhodes and George Thompson were omitted. In the party for the Test were Tom Hayward, George Gunn (whose selection in place of Rhodes *Wisden* averred a blunder), Relf, Schofield Haigh and, from Leicestershire, King and Tom Jayes, Astill's uncle. No thought was given to the incomparable but contumacious and, at times, even rebarbative Sydney Barnes.

Newspapers and public opinion were most vociferous over the omission of Jessop and Walter Brearley, the right-arm Lancashire fast bowler who was enjoying a splendid season, and the inclusion of King and Jayes, although *Cricket*, while orthodox over Jayes, defended King's selection as 'a very happy one. It is always advisable to have a sound left-handed batsman in the side, and when there is available one who has been showing good form, and one, moreover, who is a very useful bowler, what is more natural than he should be picked. Of King it may truly be said that if he had been associated with a more prominent county his real worth would have been appreciated more as it deserved to be.'

On the first morning only Leveson Gower and MacLaren were left to make the final decision. Allen Synge surmises that 'Shrimp' Leveson Gower, having allowed himself to be overawed by MacLaren in the selection for the First Test, was now determined to assert himself. It is, however, difficult to know who thought exactly what: in a letter to Jessop, MacLaren says that he had wanted both him and Brearley in the team, whereas in his autobiography Leveson Gower writes: 'I thought at the time, and still think, that it was a mistake [to omit Brearley], though the captain disagreed with me'. MacLaren also told George Beldam that he had been thwarted, presumably by Leveson Gower, over Jayes. There was also probably an element of complacency about selection, for England had won the First Test by the very comfortable margin of ten wickets and the Australians had fared poorly in the interim. That Test had, moreover, been won largely by two left-arm bowlers, Hirst and Blythe, who had taken all twenty Australian wickets between them. At Edgbaston, however, the pitch had been damp, whereas at Lord's, although it had been under water two days previously, it was hard if not good. A fast right-arm bowler was needed to bring the ball into the right-handed batsmen down the slope. Fortuitously Brearley was present. Shortly before play was due to commence he was approached; but, his *amour propre* wounded through his initial omission, he declined the invitation on the excuse that his kit was already in Tonbridge and refused to wire for it. He then, as Synge writes, 'hovered around the ground like a kind of Cassandra', stationing himself under Leveson Gower's box and crooning what he would have done had he been playing, until a policeman moved him on for carolling too soon before Christmas. Three days later his county match began at Tonbridge, where he took twelve for 117.

Thus the obvious choice to open the bowling with Hirst was Tom Jayes, that lion-hearted right-arm fast bowler and brilliant outfielder who had appeared against the Australians for an England XI in 1905, and for the Players, and was now enjoying a splendid season. But Jayes was sent home, whereat the *Daily Express* proclaimed that the feeling of disquietude among 'the majority of the cricket public . . . grew into something like hopelessness'. Poor Jayes was never to play Test cricket, and died four years later of tuberculosis after a long illness. King, therefore, on 14 June, became the first Leicestershire cricketer to play in a home Test and only the third overall.[29] Coincidentally supporters of Birkenhead Park could also pride themselves on the third of their four England players: curiously all of them were vouchsafed a single match, although Thomas Routledge was selected four times for South Africa.[30]

Obloquy was poured at the time on the selectors for their choice of King to share the opening overs with Hirst. In 1921, in its appreciation of King, *The Cricketer* bluntly asserted that this was 'a compliment which, useful bowler though he is, was scarcely deserved'. Today, when not to begin with two fast bowlers is considered lunacy, this selection is condemned even more. But it can be defended, at least to a degree. In 1909, when the uncovered pitches allowed much greater variety of tactics, a slow bowler often opened. Blythe, who was slower than King, had done so at Edgbaston, on an admittedly more favourable wicket. King, as we have seen, was not really slow, and he expressed a preference for

---

29 At the time he will have been considered the second after Knight (who had played in three of the matches of the tour of Australia in 1903/04); for the first, the all-rounder Dick Pougher, had played (and successfully, dismissing three of the first six batsmen in the order for 26 runs in the only innings in which he bowled) in the county's second-class days for W.W.Read's England team against South Africa at Cape Town in 1891/92, when such matches were deemed of lowly status. Indeed he was best known by the cricketing fraternity for his return of five wickets for no runs for MCC against the Australians at Lord's in 1896.

30 T.W.Routledge's Test appearances were at King's future home ground in South Africa, Newlands, in the only Test of the 1891/92 season, and then in the three Tests of the 1895/96 season, on all of which occasions he opened the batting for his adopted country. He never played any first-class cricket in England, although he was a member of the South African side which toured the British Isles in 1894. The other three Birkenhead players besides King to play for England were Sandford Schultz (later Storey) who was born in Birkenhead and schooled, like King's father and grandson, at Uppingham; Reginald Wood, who was born in Cheshire and played briefly for Lancashire before emigrating to Australia, where he was co-opted into the England team for the Second Test of the 1886/87 season at Melbourne; and Norman Oldfield, who was born in Cheshire, played for Lancashire and Northamptonshire and scored 80 in the Oval Test of 1939 against the West Indies, and who played for the club after his first-class career had ended.

opening when the ball was still hard. Indeed of the 33 occasions hitherto when he had taken five or more wickets in an innings 18, including one the previous week, had been when he had opened.[31] He regularly shared the new ball for Leicestershire, often with his slower colleague Astill: on one occasion the two dismissed their opponents unchanged, a feat that, with different partners, he was to accomplish in consecutive innings in 1912.

On the wicket for this match, however, the decision, even without the benefit of hindsight, was clearly wrong: Brearley should have been in the original fourteen, and on the morning Jayes was an obviously correct selection. The choice, however, should not have been, if it was indeed as the public thought, between Jayes and King: both should have played. The man to be left out ought to have been Hayward, who had been troubled by his knee in the First Test and played now against medical advice: he made but few runs and was a disaster in the field. However poorly it was actually to perform in this match, on paper the batting was strong. Hayward could have been spared, especially since Jayes was no buffoon with the bat and did actually have a first-class century to his name. We can even consider another possibility – Jayes for Haigh, a wet-wicket specialist.

So the match began, with England having what Sir Home Gordon asseverated was 'the most irrepresentative side that has ever taken the field in this country', 'a candle' in comparison with 'the sun' which had won at Edgbaston; and of which the Australian captain Monty Noble said 'Armstrong and I agreed that if we could not beat the team we had better sell our kits'. Noble won the toss and inserted his opponents, rightly judging that the wicket would dry further and be more conducive to batting on the second day. Laver and Cotter dismissed Hayward, Hobbs and Gunn and England was struggling at 44 for three when King joined Johnny Tyldesley, who had been kept very quiet. In an hour and 25 minutes they put on 79, working 'very hard for their runs', before the Lancastrian was lbw to Laver. King went on to make the top score of 60 – exactly equalling his score against the same opponents for his county two weeks before – with six boundaries out of 131 in 155 minutes.[32] Then, 'in trying to cut [Cotter] he got the ball rather too high up on his bat, and gave Macartney, at point, a catch about as swift as

---

31   The figures for his whole career are 44 out of 69.
32   His innings was the second highest at the time in a Test Match by a Leicestershire player, after Knight's unbeaten 70 at Melbourne in 1903/04.

lightning, but the little man seized the chance with the avidity and alacrity of a smart boy playing snap', as 'J.C.' reported in the *Sporting Chronicle*. King could reasonably have expected four runs from that final ball in an innings which had been hitherto chanceless. *Wisden* asserts that 'The highest and best innings was played by King, who not only showed the value of left-handed batting, but did much to justify his selection. He played a good strong game, hitting cleanly on the off-side and placing the ball well to leg', strokes which elsewhere are described as 'delightful'. 'J.C.' more colourfully declared that 'there was English beef behind his bat – and English beef was showing its superiority to Australian mutton'. England was all out by six o'clock for 269, and Hirst and King could make no inroads against McAlister and Laver that evening; but the day's play later enabled the *Leicester Daily Mercury* to delight in reprinting other newspapers' contumelious comments on King's selection together with their contrite eulogies of his performance.

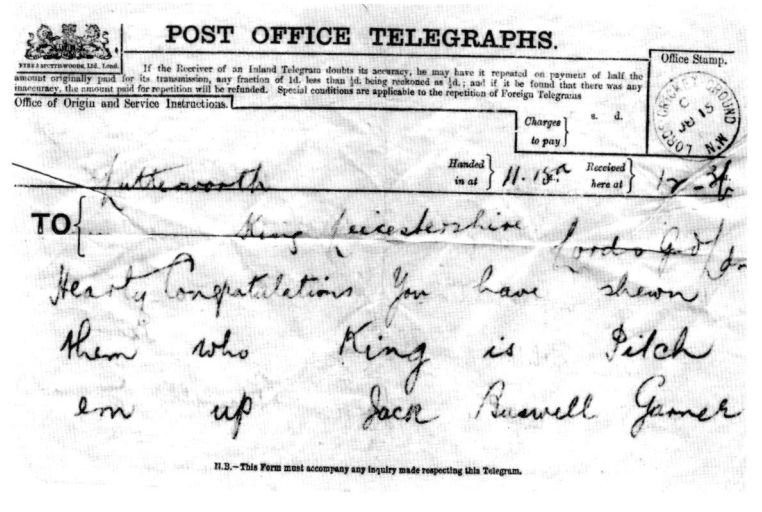

Telegram sent by a Lutterworth supporter congratulating King on his Test innings of 60.

Although the wicket had rolled out very well the next day, Australia struggled at first, losing three wickets for 90. One was that of McAlister who was lbw to King. The game was then transformed by a splendid 143 not out by Victor Ransford to give the Australians a first-innings advantage of 81 runs. But what might have been? In the course of one over King, who had taken the wicket of Ransford at Leicester for 13, had him missed in the slips by MacLaren on the same score; and then watched as Hayward dropped Trumper off his bowling before he had scored. *Wisden* records that he 'at one point bowled extremely well, but he never got over the disappointment of seeing' these blunders in the field.

On the third day England suffered ignominious defeat, being dismissed in the second innings on a good wicket for a mere 121, after which Australia easily knocked off the requisite runs for the loss of Bardsley. (A full scorecard can be seen at Appendix Two to this book.) Although King made only four, he could perhaps have taken some consolation in the fact that he was dismissed by the principal destroyer, Warwick Armstrong, who bowled him with a superb ball that came back up the slope. Since Armstrong was a leg-break bowler and he was bowling from the Nursery End, Gideon Haigh comments that 'it appears . . . Armstrong was the first Australian to bowl a wrong 'un in England, turning Bosanquet's weapon back on its creators'. The Australian captain M.A.Noble confirms that the ball was a 'wrong-un', that is 'the off-spin with the leg-break action'. Armstrong bowled two batsmen in this way – the other was Hirst – but King was the first, thus giving Leicestershire an unlikely, and unwelcome, double. Sam Coe had, of course, been the first batsman in first-class cricket to be dismissed by a googly; in 1900, he was stumped for 98 by W.P.Robertson, just short of his first first-class century, off Bosanquet, with a ball that bounced, according to reports, four times.

King was not called upon to bowl again; nor to play for England again. Lord Hawke came home from France, chaired the selectorial meetings once more, ignored his batting and perhaps made a decision based more on King's figures than reports of his bowling, which he had not of course himself witnessed.

The whole muddle-headed selection is nicely summed up by A.A.Thomson: 'It could be said, without flogging a dead horse too hard, that . . . the selectors went mad and England in the Second Test went into battle with only one fast bowler; the only batsmen to put up a fight being the wicket-keeper, Lilley, and J.H.King, who, though a medium-slow bowler, opened the bowling with Hirst, made top score . . . and was never picked for England again. For the third game the selectors dropped King, the only man who had batted well, and brought in Jack Sharp, the eminent Everton footballer, as a fast bowler. It now seems natural in this Alice-in-Wonderland rubber that Sharp should have bowled only one over, but have made top score.' Nevertheless King had once more earned his congratulatory letters and telegrams. It was perhaps on this occasion, though possibly for one of his later performances, that some poetaster – a certain 'D.C.L. of Narborough House, Leamington' – penned the following eminently forgettable quatrain:

> Knigly [sic] and great, renowned afar,
> In every clime your praises are.
> Now listen to your subjects' cheer,
> Great monarch of old Leicestershire.

King was perhaps lucky to have been selected for England in the first place; he was certainly unlucky never to be selected again.

A hand-drawn cartoon sent to King.

Chapter Eight
Maturity

On 15 May 1910, the day before the opening match of the season, King wrote the following letter to the newly appointed county secretary:

> Mr Packer
>
> Dear Sir,
>
> Having met with an accident on Sat. I shall not be able to take part in the match to-morrow. My Physician ordering me to bed. Please to acquaint the Committee & Sir Arthur Hazelerigg. Trusting it will be fine for you & that the gate will be all that is disired. Shall be anxious to see the papers to-morrow night and sincerely trust our team may be victorious. Hoping soon to be well again.
>
> Yours very truly,
>
> Jho H. King.
>
> P.S. I might mention it is my knee. The cartilage being affected.

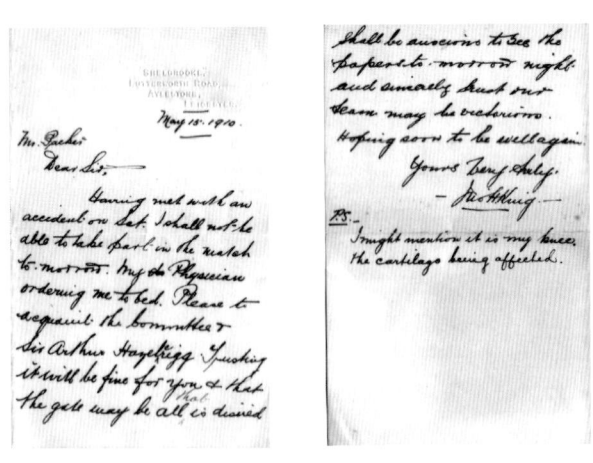

Between equals.
King's sick note to the new Leicestershire secretary, S.C. Packer.

A letter was considered an 'icon of the soul' by the Byzantines, Michael Psellos, the great polymath of the eleventh century, once going so far as to write that he could ascertain more of a man's character from a letter than from a personal meeting. What can we, more modestly, learn of King from this, the only surviving document written by him?

Although we may infer from the careful writing and use of personal embossed stationery that this was originally intended as the letter to be sent to Mr Packer, the facts that it was preserved among his daughter's memorabilia of her father and that it contains two corrections *supra lineam* in King's hand, the second inked 'e' in the name of his captain Sir Arthur Hazlerigg (the first should have been stroked out) and the pencilled 'that' in 'all that is', suggest that this became merely a draft, thereby indicating that he was conscientious and did not wish the secretary to consider him slovenly. He may, however, not have been obsessively conscientious if he was willing to allow one alteration to stand when he changed his mind after the first two letters of 'doctor' (stroked out) and penned the grander 'Physician' (unless he determined at that early stage that this was not to be his final version).

The hand is fluent and graceful, without the floridity often associated with the 1870s when he learned his penmanship, although he does permit himself a formalized paraph. The hand is similar, then, to what we know of his batting. The composition is that of a tolerably well-educated man. The grammar, especially the fondness for the present participle and the correct use of 'shall' rather than 'will', and even the punctuation, which defies the concept of a sentence, are typical of the period, while 'Jho' is a not uncommon Victorian abbreviation which has usually been taken as standing for the Latin Johannes, although scholarly doubt has recently been cast on that theory. There is but a single orthographic error, 'disired', apart from the mis-spelling of his captain's name.

Nothing should be read into the formal salutation and closing formula, since these are standard for the period, and would have probably been the same even if he had known the secretary for many years. The burden of his communication shows complete self-confidence: he cannot play, and feels no need either to seek the club's permission not to appear or to apologise for what he cannot help. Only as an afterthought does he think fit to apprise the club of the specific reason for his medical incapacity. He will have been confident that nobody would accuse him of malingering: his daughter remembered an occasion in a later year when he made use of a runner on account of a large and very painful carbuncle on his neck, whose lancing did not preclude his playing the following day; and the common reaction to muscular sprains was simply a hot bath with perhaps an application of liniment before the morrow's play. This was probably preferable to the 'treatment' remembered by various county players directly after the Second World War who preferred not to mention their pains for fear of a pummelling on the trainer's table.

It is notable, finally, that King puts first his hopes for a good gate, with which a secretary would be most concerned, and only second his own anxious desire for his county's success, although he expatiates on the latter. This is a letter written as from equal to equal, which was not the typical relationship before the Great War for a county secretary, albeit one only very recently appointed and a paid employee. Now an England player, he was unostentatiously conscious of his own worth.

King's trust that Leicestershire would be victorious was justified, his hope for his own speedy recovery not fulfilled.

S.C.Packer, Leicestershire's secretary from 1910 to 1932.

The injury unfortunately prevented him from playing in his benefit match, in late June, against neighbouring Nottinghamshire, which Leicestershire, batting on a damaged pitch after the opposition's opening 336, lost by seven wickets. King's consolation came from gates of £55 2s 9d, £7 3s 0d and £46 1s 3d which, when swelled by donations, resulted in an eventual sum for him of £275 19s 4d. As for the paltry sum on the second day, 'Reynard' wrote that King, 'as one who rejoices in a garden . . . would welcome today's gentle rain, as the beneficiaire . . . he would have preferred a continuance of the spell of dry weather. His roses and sweet peas might have drooped under the drought, but the "gate" would not have been so thin.'

Pages from the bank statement for King's benefit match in June, 1910. The final sum was a modest £276, equivalent to £20,500 at 2009 prices.

The committee gave him also £1 10s 0d as 'talent money' this year, even though his cricket was restricted to two matches: he batted with some success against both Yorkshire and Lancashire, including 'a gallant show' of 60 at Leeds, before being bowled by his bête-noire Hirst, to help bring a rare victory over the 'Tykes'; but he bowled only six overs for a single wicket in the two games. Surgery was necessary. His daughter claimed that he had to pay an extra guinea to ensure that he was operated on with gloves; and his caution paid off since there was no infection and he was fit for the start of the following season and performed some of his most memorable feats in the next four years until the outbreak of war.

The season of 1910 saw the début of a man from George Geary's birthplace of Barwell, a certain Albert Callington, who jocularly insisted on being known throughout his career by the surname of Lord (as he appears on all scorecards and in all newspaper reports) on the ground that the county already had a Knight and a King.[33] It is unknown whether it gave King any qualms by drawing attention to the meaning of his name, which probably originated as either a similar crotchet or from the rôle in a pageant play, in light of the local superstition, known from the early 1300s, that 'misfortune would attend any king who entered the town of Leicester', a prognostication probably based upon the fates of Edmund Ironside, Harold Godwinson, William II and Edward II and kept alive by those of many subsequent monarchs.[34] He was, of course, aware of his putative descent from Robert I, king of the Scots, since he named his daughter Margaret Bruce. Lord's whimsicality was picked up in one stanza of Arthur B.Talbot's 'A New Bawl' in praise of the county's cricketing heroes which was published in the club's Jubilee Souvenir of 1928:

> For years of all-round service we must sing
> A verse of gratitude to J.H.King.
> Four Kings in turn are seen upon the sward,
> A Knight of cut and thrust, and eke a Lord.
> And lo, we cry 'What oh!' to Sammy Coe,
> 'And may his shadow never smaller grow.'

33　This whimsicality extended, according to Tom Belton, an elderly resident of Barwell, even to members of the county cricketer's family playing in village games.

34　In the 1881 Census, the surname King, though not anywhere rare, was most commonly found in South-East England rather than in the East Midlands.

Maturity

King's return to continuous cricket in 1911 was on the whole moderate. His 1,187 runs were scored at an average of 28.95, and his 73 wickets were expensive at 31.42 each, although early on the local paper claimed that his 'cunning of hand and brain has evidently not suffered from his enforced idleness last year'. Two feats stand out. The first is simply a statistical anomaly. A century against Lancashire was in those days always a notable performance, but in his 'resolute and sound' 103 not out at Old Trafford, King reached 96 with 14 fours and 40 singles without ever making a hit for two or three. He then cut a ball for two before ending with another single and another four to bring up his century. The second feat is one of the most outstanding individual achievements in the county's history.

Mighty Yorkshire, though winning one of the matches, encountered magnificent opposition from the minnows of Leicestershire this year. At Bradford C.J.B.Wood carried his bat for a century in each innings, a feat not equalled until the South African S.J.Cook performed it again for Somerset in 1989. At the conclusion of the match George Hirst is reported to have entered the visitors' dressing-room and exclaimed 'Mr Wood, when we come to Leicester for the return match, I'll bring a pistol and, if we can't bowl you out, we'll shoot you'. But at Aylestone Road it was King who was principally responsible for his county's solitary victory of the season, and that by an innings, an unique performance for the county over these opponents at the time. On a day of rioting in Glasgow in the tramwaymen's strike, Yorkshire, facing a deficit of 67, was at one point 22 for one and later 37 for two wickets, before being humiliated on a damaged pitch drying out under a hot sun for a total of 47. Although the 'pitch had come to the help of Leicestershire as Blucher did to Wellington at Waterloo ... Leicestershire had outplayed the Tykes from the very beginning of the match. ... I have never', crowed the reporter in the *Leicester Daily Mercury*, 'seen Leicestershire more melancholy, more glaringly in a state of collapse than the Yorkshire team were this morning. ... Six [sic] ducks at a sitting ! Vae victis !' The *Leeds Mercury* was perhaps even more damning: 'the capitulation was inglorious and undignified, no fewer than seven members of the side being dismissed without scoring, which must surely be a record for the county'.

King's analysis of eight for 17 in this débâcle was remarkable enough, but his last seven wickets were taken in a mere 20 balls

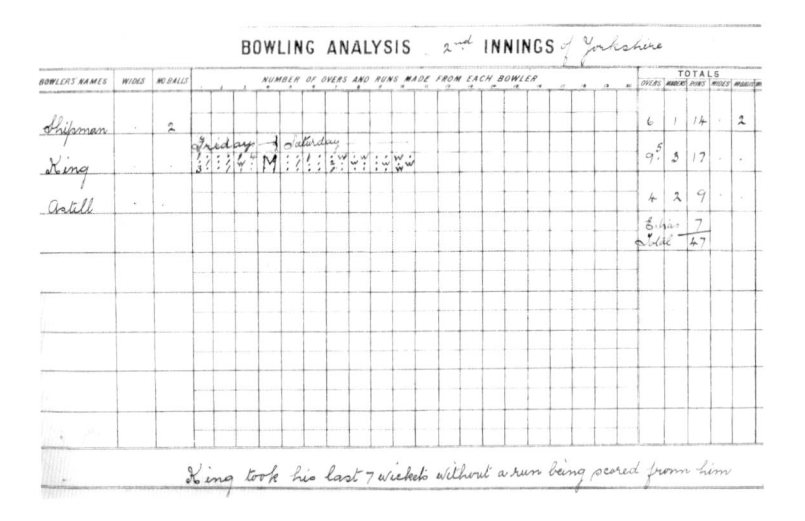

The Leicestershire scorebook showing King's best first-class bowling return, eight for 17 against Yorkshire in August 1911, including seven wickets in twenty balls.
The book seems to have been 'copied up' after the event.

The county's grandees solemnly gather for a formal presentation to King and C.J.B.Wood for their performances in Leicestershire's matches against Yorkshire in 1911.
King took 8 for 17 in the home match and Wood twice carried his bat for centuries at Bradford.

without a run conceded. Only Grace, in 1877, had ever taken seven wickets in fewer balls (17); and, although C.H.Palmer later took eight wickets for the county without conceding a run against Surrey in 1955, his first seven took him 47 balls.[35] Yorkshire's collapse in losing eight wickets for ten runs – declining from 37 for two to 47 all out – was, however, statistically less dramatic than one surprisingly little-remembered in Leicestershire's last match of the 1951 season. In that match seven Lancashire wickets fell, again to spin (on this occasion that of Jackson and Munden), for the addition of only two leg-byes (towards the end, however, at least two easy runs were turned down by the bewildered and demoralized batsmen); but, with the onset of rain, that collapse did not ensure a victory for Leicestershire.

Other fine performances this season pale into insignificance, but it should be mentioned that, at Aylestone Road, King scored centuries on good pitches against Sussex and Hampshire, in the former match gathering fours as 'plentiful as blackberries', and in the latter showing a mastery now over the googly and being

---

35 Palmer's eight took him 63 balls, King's eight required 47, but the latter had nine runs scored off him between the taking of the first and second wicket.

unperturbed by the antics of its purveyor H.A.H.Smith, who 'has a fantastic little run to the wicket, with a back-kick of the leg just before delivering the ball, like a naughty ballet-dancer'. In sterner contests he defied Surrey, also at home, with a chanceless 93 not out 'in his very finest punishing style', and battled against Blythe at Dover with a top score of 21 followed by a defiant 49 not out. He had five-wicket hauls in the first, second and fourth home matches of the season (against Lancashire, Kent and Worcestershire), but thereafter his bowling tailed away except for that one extraordinary match.[36]

In 1912 King took 130 wickets at an average of 17.63. This was 57 wickets more for one run fewer than in the previous season and 49 more than he had ever taken before. His total was at the time the highest taken by a Leicestershire player (though not in county games alone); while his average was the lowest since the pre-first class days of Pougher in the early 1890s, and has been beaten, up to the present day, only by George Geary, in his case three times. Match after match he seemed to take five wickets in an innings, sixteen times in all, more than double his previous best of seven in 1900. The weather was abominable and the pitches often 'soft and dead', but he 'developed a quality of absolute genius for bowling on this sort of wicket'. In its summation of the season the *Leicester Daily Mercury* averred that 'he is now a more consummate master of attack than ever before in all his brilliant career. ... His artifice is more varied; his judgment more subtly calculated. Always one of the most intelligent trundlers, he has never bowled badly throughout the summer.' Since he also scored over 1,000 runs, albeit at the low average of 22.85 (but second in the Championship averages at 24.21), the strain on the stamina of a man now in his forty-second year must have been enormous. His 'double', though dependent upon a few runs for MCC, was the first achieved by a Leicestershire player. Yet his county finished only thirteenth in the table. The explanation is easy to see: 32 of his wickets were taken out of the Championship in which he and Astill took nearly 68% of the wickets to fall to bowlers (171 out of 253; while against the two touring teams the pair took a further 19 out of 29, 16 of them to

---

36   In the Worcestershire match King was injured in a very odd way. In the first innings, according to *Scores and Biographies*, 'when he was bowled by R.D.Burrows, the ball struck the stumps with such force that a bail shot forward and cut his face near the left eye: the wound bled for some time, but he was able to take his place in the field when Worcestershire went in.' Indeed he opened the bowling and put up a performance that *Wisden* considered superior even to that of Burrows, who then proceeded to win the match for the visitors.

King). The only other bowlers whose tally of wickets was in double figures were Bill Shipman with 27 at huge cost and Jack Curtis with 12.

His season opened and closed with five-wicket hauls, for MCC against Yorkshire (to counterbalance his 'spectacles' from Hirst) and for his county against Lancashire. In between these hauls two bowling feats stand out statistically. Kent's visit to Aylestone Road was Blythe's match, the master taking 15 wickets for 45 on a highly treacherous pitch with seven for 9 in the home team's lowest-ever innings of 25, but King, opening the bowling, hit back with eight for 26, which he followed with a resolute 49, his county's top score, in the second innings. *Wisden* comments that 'In view of the state of the game, King's achievement almost equalled Blythe's'. The other feat was again in a losing cause, this time against the visiting South Africans. His analyses were five for 52 and seven for 45, thus pipping Aubrey Faulkner's total for the match by one. In the second innings he dismissed the first four batsmen in the order, L.J.Tancred, H.W.Taylor, A.W.Nourse and Faulkner, who made only 15 runs between them, the openers both being stumped by John Shields. The local correspondent even believed that he bowled some deliveries that 'actually broke the other way to his usual one' (i.e. off-breaks to the right-handers). One other match provided him with ten wickets (for 117 runs against Derbyshire at Ashby-de-la-Zouch in 62.4 overs). In addition he twice he took seven wickets in an innings (*v* Kent at Dover and Warwickshire at Hinckley). In two consecutive innings in June he and Astill bowled out the opposition unchanged (*v* Worcestershire at Stourbridge in a rain-ruined match limited to a single innings each side and in the first innings *v* Warwickshire at Nuneaton to help their county to victory by a meagre three runs). Indeed this pair of spin bowlers, left- and right-handed, frequently opened the bowling; and King himself was entrusted with the new ball in every match but two, in one of which by reason of rain the opposition never batted. And he was not given long spells only when the wicket suited him: seven times he bowled at least 35 overs in an innings, the most being 58 against Nottinghamshire at Leicester and 53 (with a further 23 in the second innings) for MCC against Oxford University.

In view of all this bowling (some 930 six-ball overs in the season) it is a measure of the strength and determination of this elderly cricketer that he had any energy at all left for batting. Nonetheless, despite his rigours in the field, he scored an unbeaten and chanceless century in the home match against Worcestershire, shepherding an abject tail after he and Wood had put on 131 together; and made a dogged unbeaten 86 in a losing cause at Southampton straight after bowling 39.5 overs in which he took five wickets for 114.

An improvement of nearly 17 in his batting average in 1913 must be weighed against a decline of nearly 20 in that for bowling: indeed he took a mere 27 wickets (all in the Championship). I can find no properly satisfactory explanation for this deterioration, which affected Astill also, though to a lesser degree, and *Wisden* is no help herein. He had been engaged to coach the young members at the start of the season, but he can hardly have been jaded. More likely reasons are that the wickets were drier and therefore less suitable for King, and that the county gave extended and successful trials to two new opening bowlers, George Geary and Alec Skelding, while a third, Bill Shipman, recovered his form. They were all, however, somewhat expensive, and Leicestershire dropped a position (although this disappointment must have palled in comparison with the relief felt at escaping that winter from a financial crisis that threatened the county club's very existence). King only once took as many as four wickets in an innings – and they were expensive at 104 runs (against Lancashire at Leicester).

In the first half of the season he batted respectably, his 80 at Southampton ensuring with Harry Whitehead safety and 66 against Nottinghamshire promising the salvation that was promptly lost on his dismissal; but his best innings was probably a 'masterly' top-score of 37 out of 97 (before he was caught off his glove) in which he for once defied a rampant Hirst whose trickiness was aided by a strong crosswind. His three centuries all came in the space of a fortnight in August. First, directly following his saving of a game against the 'Peakites' with an 'assured' 82, in a drawn game on an easy pitch at Aylestone Road he took 111 and 100* off Northamptonshire with sixteen fours in each innings, the first 'in one of his brightest moods', with 'splendidly-timed off-drives' and 'grace and accuracy of cutting'. This was the second time, after Wood's marvellous performance two years earlier, that this feat of two hundreds in a match had been accomplished for the county, and also the second time for King after his double for the Players. Nonetheless, his highest innings of the year was more valuable: Leicestershire was forced to follow on at Worcester, but

Maturity

King's unbeaten 146 in four and a half hours of 'clean driving' and 'crisp cutting' allied with judicious defence begun in the 'pronounced gloom' of the second evening gave Skelding the opportunity to bring about a sensational victory by a mere eight runs. In his two matches against the 'Sauce County' King had a total aggregate of 330. His late-season form brought him selection for an England XI at Harrogate, where he top-scored with 45 first time round and again managed to evade Hirst, this time in both innings.

The Leicestershire side of 1913, which finished fourteenth of sixteen in the Championship.
Standing (l to r): S.C.Packer (secretary), unknown, A.Lord, F.Osborn, A.Mounteney, A.Skelding and G.Geary.
Seated: C.J.B.Wood, W.Shipman, J.Shields (captain and wk), J.H.King and W.E.Astill.
On the ground: W.N.Riley, H.Whitehead, W.Brown.

Despite having a record similar to that of the previous year Leicestershire generally performed better in 1914. This was due in considerable extent to Geary's emergence as a first-class bowler, but King's return to form in this discipline must not be discounted and it helped to give his county 'almost an embarrassment of riches in the matter of attack'. His average in Championship matches was 21.51 for 62 wickets, while he averaged over 14 runs better in his batting for well over 1,000 runs.

As if determined to show that he was still a bowler with whom to be reckoned, he ran through the Essex second innings in the

Maturity

opening match with five for only 26 in 19 overs of 'puzzling spin' to bring his side a very comfortable victory, and had the personal satisfaction of bowling the opener Russell between his legs and twice dismissing the opposing captain, J.W.H.T.Douglas, then at the height of his form. And he will have been even more pleased with claiming Jack Hobbs in both innings at Loughborough, caught each time by that brilliant fielder Harry Whitehead. Nevertheless, despite further five-wicket hauls at Birmingham and Bradford (in both of which matches he took eight wickets in all) he faded later in the year and was frequently little used.

Perhaps his most valuable innings for his club was an 'obdurate' 71 against Lancashire which helped to bring a rare and narrow victory over this opposition – and a reward of £5 from a Mr Ernest Clarke of Kilby Bridge, who had deposited the cheque with the secretary for the first batsman to reach 50 in the second innings. In contrasting mood for a score of similar magnitude he hit with some gusto in making 70 out of 91 while he was at the wicket in a losing cause against Fielder, Blythe and Woolley at Ashby-de-la-Zouch. His three centuries were all outstanding in different ways. First, in early June, he scored his only century against Yorkshire, an undefeated 114 on a drying pitch against an otherwise regnant Hirst (five for 94) out of 241. He gave only one chance in four hours and, after the opening hour brought him but a single, 'hit freely' in 'forc[ing] the game with as much resolution as was possible, consistent with reasonable safety' to give his side a first-innings lead for the first of two times in the season against his inveterate foes. In August at Northampton on a soft, rain-affected wicket his 124, over half of the total of 228 (212 from the bat), was a masterly, though not faultless, exhibition 'of sound defence mingled with intermittent audacity', while in the second innings an extra boundary added to his 24 out of 79 would have tied a thrilling match of low scores in which Leicestershire missed the services the second time round of A.T.Sharp who was called up for military duties. King's third century marked a red-letter day in his career.

On the outskirts of Coalville, a mining town so dominated by its industry that its name had been changed from Long Lane, a ground had been fashioned on the Boulder Clay over the ubiquitous Mercia Mudstone opposite the Fox and Goose Hotel, after which it was named; and it was well named, for in the county's only two games on the ground, against Worcestershire in this and the preceding year, the Leicestershire predator mercilessly tormented and then destroyed its prey. In 1914, after the visitor's dismissal for 223, King was able to reach 55 by the close of the opening day. On the Monday (13 July) he and Harry Whitehead (103) improved their third-wicket partnership to 150 at a steady pace. Then, with the more aggressive Coe (76), he enjoyed an exhilarating partnership of 159 in under two hours before having to shepherd an unproductive tail. His chanceless and undefeated innings, characterized by 33 boundaries all round the wicket, lasted six and a quarter hours and finally reached 227, the highest score of his career and, at the time, bettered for Leicestershire only by Knight's 229* against the same county in 1903 and, just six weeks previously, by Coe's belligerent 252* against Northamptonshire.

King's highest first-class score recorded in Storer Taylor's neat hand.

It is even to-day the third highest innings for Leicestershire by a left-hander and, sad commentary on the modern lack of county loyalties, still the third highest Championship score by a Leicestershire-born player. With 'a chanceless' 90 and 'a dazzling' 71* the previous year, though hampered by a leg-sprain, King had made a total of 388 runs for once out in the two matches on this ground (and Whitehead, with his earlier 100 and 68, had made 271); but the pitch was by no means a featherbed, for on it Geary, with 11 wickets in each match, dismissed 22 Worcestershire batsmen for only 229 runs. The 'Sauce Men' must have been tired of King: in the four matches of 1913 and 1914 he had scored 607 runs against them at an average of 202.33.

The last match of the season, at The Oval, was cancelled because of the outbreak of war, and King's mother died very shortly thereafter (in September), having been able to follow what surely, as the war continued its seemingly interminable and destructive course, all followers of the game must have considered her son's entire career in first-class cricket.

Chapter Nine
Interlude

Upon the outbreak of war King did not enlist. Why should he? The war in its early months was expected to be a short and triumphant adventure for a gay and gallant band of youngsters, and King was past 43. Great Britain was the only European country involved in the Great War not to introduce early conscription, for the government feared exacerbating the split in opinion of the Cabinet, some of whose members disliked fighting 'the industrious, respectable ant' of Germany in defence of 'the decadent and frivolous grasshopper' of France, in Tuchman's memorable phrases.

When conscription was finally introduced, in early 1916, it was only for men up to the age of 41. Later, however, upon the raising of the maximum age he was indeed called up, but the verdict delivered at the Glen Parva barracks was 'Mr King is not a fighting man and would be much more use on the home front'. He consequently did work on the farm of a Mr Custouce on the Narborough Road, south of the village of that name, cycling every day from Aylestone via Coalpit Lane. The County Ground had meanwhile been commandeered by the Army, the pavilion

Total war.
The Army Service Corps on parade at the Aylestone Road ground, probably in 1915.

Interlude

becoming the headquarters of the 53rd ASC Remount Depot and the playing area a drill-ground for the Leicestershire Volunteer Regiment.

Sometime around the onset of war the Kings perforce moved home. Florence's sister Elizabeth, a sculptor with a studio in Madrid, returned to England and, being somewhat impecunious, moved into the parental home, 'eventually taking over our part of the house', as daughter Margaret recalled. John, Florence and Margaret consequently lived for eighteen months in a small house in Aylestone Park until they were able to purchase 551 Aylestone Road ('Rutland House'), the slightly older building attached to the parental No.549. Their new home had previously belonged to a nurseryman, most of whose sheds and greenhouses had to be removed. The groundsman from the County Ground helped in laying down and landscaping the top garden. As with father-in-law's house, the property with gardens and paddock ran down to the Grand Union Canal just east of the River Soar, and King had the boating and fishing rights between locks to north and south. At some point he also acquired shooting rights along Coalpit Lane, and, being a good shot, was able to bring home many a bird in addition to clutches of plovers' and other birds' eggs.

King with his Airedale terrier, Gypsy, outside 511 Aylestone Road in the autumn of 1914.

I can find no other trace of his life in this period apart from the fact that he stayed at home with his family until the early summer of 1918. His daughter said that when he went to work on the farm outside Narborough 'mother looked after father's business interests' but I have not been able to ascertain what these were. (At some unspecified time he worked for what his daughter called an 'oil firm' making shellac.[37]) Certainly he kept fit with digging his garden which he kept 'quite beautiful'. At no time does he seem to have had serious financial problems. He had inherited some money from his father, and his wife had brought some into the marriage. His position, then, with whatever business interests he had, was, even when he had no earnings from cricket, far superior to that of most of his fellow-professionals. He was indeed rather better off than his much later successor as Leicestershire's left-arm all-rounder, the Australian Jack Walsh, the sight upon whose mantelpiece of jars labelled 'rates', 'electricity', 'water' etc., to aid from small change the ultimate necessity of paying the respective bills, so affrighted his two fellow-countrymen Murray Sargent and Philip Saunders that they abandoned all thought of a career in English county cricket and scurried back to the Antipodes.

It seems that for the first three years of the war King played little cricket, five matches in 1915 and one in 1917 being the only ones now traceable. Nonetheless, the summer of 1918 found him as professional for Eccleshill, a place with a long history of cricket, for one Sunday in the mists of time, as legend has it, the parish clerk, also a local umpire, one Lingard by name, upon awakening from a sermon-induced slumber, confounded his neighbours' Amens with a sonorous and different term of closure – 'Over'.

In this last summer of the War Eccleshill, with four wins, eight losses and eight draws, finished 16th out of 20 in the Bradford League. King's appointment was announced in the *Bradford Daily Argus* only on 20 April: 'There was a goodly gathering of talented players, amongst whom was King, of Leicester County, Eccleshill's latest capture'. The appointment was in part 'to formulate a nursery for young players'. King came 14th in the League batting averages with 384 runs at 29.53, his highest innings being 100 and 60* in the two matches against Tong Park and 65 against Great Horton, for which last he had for a while as partner his county colleague C.J.B.Wood. His century was remarkable in that he hit 11 fours in his first 47 runs and 19 in all in his final total of 100. He was 22nd in the bowling averages with 43 wickets at 14.06, his best performance being seven wickets for 18 against Idle, and he often had opponents 'in difficulties with [his] deliveries'.

---

37   After his playing career had ended he occasionally reported himself as an 'oil merchant'.

These, though not outstanding, were no mean figures, especially for a man of 47, because, as Leslie Duckworth claims, 'It is doubtful if ever before or since there has been a higher standard of cricket in any league in the world than there was in the Bradford League at that time . . . a roll-call taken among the clubs sounded like an England team, with enough notable names left over to make a very good side for The Rest'. This 'roll-call' included Frank Woolley, J.W.Hearne, Schofield Haigh, George Gunn, David Denton, J.N.Crawford, Bill Hitch and the two non-pareils, Jack Hobbs and Sidney Barnes. As if these were not enough there were many such as Herbert Sutcliffe, Ernest Tyldesley, Cecil Parkin and Leicestershire's Alec Skelding destined to make high reputations in the ensuing decade. Of these four, all but Sutcliffe had played for their counties before the War. In total there were no fewer than 54 players with first-class experience who appeared in the Bradford League between 1914 and 1919. Matches were played in a chivalrous spirit: King himself 'walked' on at least one occasion, and was himself reprieved when the Keighley wicket-keeper acknowledged that he had not had the ball in his hands when taking off the bails.

Chapter Ten
Nestor

In comparison with some counties Leicestershire was fortunate in the matter of casualties during the War. Of regular players the only fatality was of that fine medium-paced bowler Billy Odell, who, as a second lieutenant in the Sherwood Foresters, was reported missing in the attack to secure Broodseine Ridge, near Passchendaele, in October 1917, having just been awarded the Military Cross 'for conspicuous gallantry and devotion in taking out a patrol at a critical time and gathering valuable information'; but he would have been well past his prime by 1919. Probably more serious a loss was that of the youngster W.N.Riley, who already had a century against Yorkshire to his name but now had but a single leg. Others, aspirants for county cricket before the War, had now altered their plans for life. So Leicestershire entered its first post-war season with much the same team as had fought its last campaign in 1914.

The side was led by Wood, now 43 and captain as he had been before the war; it included Coe, who would turn 46 in June, and King, who was already 48. It is no wonder that *Wisden* asserted that the county 'stands in great need of new blood'. Notwithstanding, Leicestershire was to be well served by its elderly servants between the World Wars. King played regularly until he was over 54, Astill played a few games past 51, Coe past 50, Geary regularly past 45 and de Trafford in 1920, after admittedly a break of seven years, played a single game, celebrating with a straight drive for six off V.W.C.Jupp, at the age of 56. And they were usually worth their place: after turning thirty and in spite of losing four years to the War while in his forties King scored 92.51% of his 25,122 runs and took 90.44% of his 1,204 wickets. The corresponding figures are 92.15% of 22,731 and 79.92% of 2,431 for Astill; 85.32% of 13,504 and 80.13% of 2,063 for Geary; and 81.76% of Coe's 17,367 runs. More strikingly, after turning forty King scored 47.17% of his runs and took 44.85% of his wickets; the corresponding figures being 39.78% and 37.27% for Astill, 25.20% and 21.13% for Geary and 35.95% for Coe's runs. Even these remarkable figures were to be put into the shade, however, by a 26-year-old making his début in 1919: Norman Armstrong scored one and two in his single match that year before returning to the side at the age of 32 to give him 99.98% of his 19,002 runs after the age of thirty and 57.39% after forty. King, however, had prematurely the last laugh, if that is possible, by scoring 21.55% of his runs and taking 8.55% of his wickets after passing fifty.

In this, the last phase of his active career, King had a new supporter, his daughter Margaret. The Aylestone Road ground being fortuitously on her route home, she would with a friend scamper the mile and a half or so from her grammar school as soon as they were let out. While they avidly watched the match, she would keep the scorebook for her friend whose job it was to do the homework. At home she would draw little pictures of her father's fellow cricketers for his amusement. He was, however, increasingly hampered by rheumatism. Fred Root recalls an interchange between Bill Reeves, who was officiating at Aylestone Road, and King when the latter 'appeared somewhat lame as he came in to bat'. 'What's the matter, John ? You look a bit wobbly', said the umpire, to which the batsman replied, 'Yes, William, I have a touch of rheumatism in my knees, and I get stiff when resting. I shall be all right when I get going'. Shortly afterwards Geary called for a short run and King 'had run many yards past the wicket, and towards the pavilion, in his effort to get to the crease', but before he had pulled up he heard 'Keep on going while your knees are loose, boy; you were just out'. Robertson-Glasgow reports that King 'was very angry' at Reeves' humour, which was always more waspish than that of Leicestershire's more kindly Alec Skelding.[38]

Although for the season of 1919 matches were limited to two days, the extended hours must have been a sore tribulation to Leicestershire's veterans. King's figures look poor despite him being one place above the great Maurice Tate in the national bowling averages; although it must be borne in mind that Tate was still an off-break bowler at that period. But, if one ignores his performances in his two matches against the exhilarating Australian Imperial Forces XI for Leicestershire and MCC (for whom he opened the batting against Gregory and Collins), his figures in the Championship show that his batting average was more than three runs clear of that for bowling, thus amply

---

38 This was probably Leicestershire's match with Yorkshire at Aylestone Road in 1922, when King was run out for 47.

justifying his place in a side that did remarkably well to finish equal ninth with Derbyshire and above, among others, Middlesex and Sussex.

He eased himself into first-class cricket again with 7 and 42 at Trent Bridge, after an 'impressive' memorial service conducted at the ground by the Bishop of Southwell for those cricketers who had lost their lives in the recent sanguinary conflict. Then, in the very next game, against Derbyshire, he scored 'with confidence and serenity' over 40% of his side's runs with 59 and 82. For his main contributions with the bat thereafter he dominated the first innings against Yorkshire with 'a necessarily somewhat restrained' 67 out of 161, the tail-ender J.S.Curtis scoring 34 but no other batsman more than 13; and to conclude the season made 64 at Coventry. That this last was out of a total of 285 suggests that it was nothing remarkable, but Warwickshire had just been humiliated by being bowled out (literally) for 48 and King, unusually opening the innings, promptly lost his partner Wood, bowled also (for a single), as were the next two batsmen to make 13 in a row. Then, 'with resolution against the odds', King proceeded to show his team-mates that the terrors of the pitch were, at least in part, imaginary. Fittingly he was not out at the end of the match, which Leicestershire won by ten wickets.

His best bowling came in a single week in June when he took five for 45 and three for 36 at Northampton and then six for 36 and three for 84 at home against Gloucestershire. This latter match was the first ever between these two counties, Leicestershire having been considered too humble opponents in the time of Grace and up to the great societal levelling created by the First World War. King was largely responsible for the victory, since he scored 51 in his county's first innings of 285 and then bowled unchanged with Geary to force Gloucestershire to follow on – all on the first day.

Shortly before the beginning of the 1920 season, with its return to a full programme of three-day matches, King turned 49. To the astonishment of friends and foes he took exactly 100 wickets at an average of 17.65, only two one-hundredths of a run more than in his great season of 1912. Moreover, since he did not play in any extraneous matches, every single wicket was taken in the Championship, the only time that he ever achieved that feat. With a rejuvenated Astill taking 97 wickets Leicestershire, despite record crowds to replenish the coffers, must have been disappointed to finish as low as fourteenth, but the fact that as many as seven matches were won, the second most in the county's history up to that time, indicates that there was much to admire. The weak point was batting with only three centuries scored, and King himself, with presumably little energy to spare, scored only 780 runs at 19.02, but this still allowed him the boast of achieving the all-rounder's criterion of a batting average above that for bowling.

'In great need of new blood.'
Six of this Leicestershire side in June 1920 were over forty.
Standing (l to r): S.Taylor (scorer), A.Mounteney, jun., G.Shingler, W.E.Astill, A.Skelding, H.Whitehead, W.E.Benskin and S.C.Packer (secretary).
Seated: S.Coe, C.E.de Trafford, C.J.B.Wood (captain), J.H.King and T.E.Sidwell (wk).
De Trafford, playing in his final first-class match, was 56 and, at the time, the oldest cricketer to play in the 'official' Championship.

As if knowing what was to follow, Leicestershire entrusted him with the county's first ball of the summer, against Hampshire at home, and he speedily took the first wicket and followed this up with the county's first 50, but he managed only four more of the latter, the biggest, a mere 72, being the highest innings of a low-scoring match at Northampton in which he brought his side victory by taking five second-innings wickets for 35. His finest bowling performance was a double of eight for 61 and five for 41, statistically the third-best innings and second-best match figures of his career, in an eventually comfortable victory over Derbyshire after a first-innings deficit. There were many other notable performances such as his seven for 46 and four for 52 at Old Trafford, where he got 'the ball to turn awkwardly' on a 'soft, lifeless wicket drying under the influence of a strong breeze' and only Hallows and Ernest Tyldesley in one innings each were able to puzzle him out. Although in the home match against Somerset, the first ever between the two counties, he had no wicket in the second innings, when the opposition was set only 138 to win, his parsimonious concession of only six runs off his first 12 overs (and ultimately 17 off 30) was a major contribution to his side's victory by 47 runs, as it allowed Astill to bowl with the necessary aggression to take wickets. In the return match at Weston-super-Mare, King performed the hat-trick for the second time in his career. Four of his seven wickets for 34 runs, including the 'hat-trick' ball, were to catches by Astill, who took the other three wickets in bringing about the same victorious result as in the home match two months earlier. At Derby the same two bowlers concluded their opponents' home season by dismissing them for 53 (King four for 25). When as September dawned and Leicestershire reached Southampton King need another four wickets for his century, but Hampshire put on 183 for the first wicket and he had none of the first three. The armed forces then gave him a boost as he ensnared both a major (the Hon Lionel Tennyson) and a commander (Gerald Harrison) before he clean bowled another amateur, the Cambridge Blue Harold McDonell. But the hardened professionals C.P.Mead and J.A.Newman then engaged in a long stand. When this was broken by King's partner his heart must have sunk, but, though the score was past 400, Tennyson 'chivalrously' did not declare and soon thereafter King

King's second hat-trick, off Somerset at Weston-super-Mare in 1920, was followed by a defiant six from 'Crusoe' Robertson-Glasgow.

delightedly caught an unusually aggressive Mead off his own bowling. The declaration came immediately, but King had his prize. He had also achieved what literary critics call 'ring-composition': first and last ball of the season for his county, first and last wicket.

After a very poor summer personally in 1920 Wood, increasingly troubled by lumbago, resigned as captain, and played only a further three games for his county. It is likely that King, rather than Wood, would have been captain for the last few years, but for the convention of an amateur captain which was to endure for many years yet. (Leicestershire first broke with tradition with Astill's appointment in 1935, but then, after a gloriously successful year under his leadership, promptly sacked him for the amateur C.S.Dempster and further years of obscurity). Even more than for the past decade and a half King was now the wise elder statesman and confidant of the younger players and one, moreover, who could still perform worthy feats, another Nestor – albeit without the Pylian's garrulity and capacity for wine. After the inter-regnum of A.T.Sharp in 1921 King was quasi-captain through the reign of Major G.H.S.Fowke. His daughter had a splendid memory of Lord Hawke, that stickler for the proprieties, loudly upbraiding King for his chalcenterous breach of custom when he espied him descending the steps from the amateurs' dressing room, whereupon the amateurs vociferously defended King on the ground that they themselves had invited him to their sanctum because they had needed his advice.

Already for some years before the outbreak of war King had been senior professional and, though in accordance with custom sitting down first and carving while his fellow-professionals waited for him to begin eating before venturing to do the same themselves, he never abused his position or caused any grievance or animosity to be directed against himself. He was certainly well suited for this rôle of senior statesman, for he was a highly experienced player, unselfish, skilled in both batting and bowling and a noted fielder, at least in his earlier years. He was, moreover, a thoughtful student of the game, wise to the devices of his opponents, able personally to adapt to the exigencies of changing situations during a match, and always willing to impart advice quietly but with great acuity to younger colleagues. By temperament he was a mild man, but one with high standards of behaviour. He smoked a pipe, which for some reason always gave a greater impression of quiet assurance, reliability, honesty and sage discernment than a flamboyantly self-advertising cigar and a self-consciously sophisticated, nervously excited or incogitantly proletarian cigarette. And he drank with great moderation: 'he did not think much' of his team-mates William Benskin and Arthur Mounteney, whom at home he deprecatingly styled 'beer-swillers', as his daughter observed. Moreover, he was loyal to his family, his friends and his county. Indeed, in a manner reminiscent of Hambledon's members sporting buttons engraved with the letters 'CC', he even had his own waistcoat buttons especially made with a miniature fox's mask in each to show his devotion to the hunting county whose cricket team still vaunts its vulpine emblem. When he told a reporter from the *Leicester Mercury* in 1923 that he had 'always enjoyed his cricket in his long connection with Leicestershire' it was no platitudinous parochial patriotism.

One of King's vulpine waistcoat buttons.

Having shown what he could do with the ball at the age of 49, King now showed, though suffering periodically from rheumatism, what he could do with the bat at 50, demonstrating 'the skill and power' and the 'plent[iful] variety' of scoring strokes of old in obtaining three centuries and six fifties in his nearly fifteen hundred runs. His 1,000 was reached on 2 July, only just over halfway through the season. He still bowled sufficiently to take 55 wickets at an average two below his batting, but this was the last year in which he could be classed as an all-rounder. It was Astill's great bowling year: he established a new county record of 152 Championship wickets and became the first Leicestershire cricketer to emulate King by achieving the 'double'. Since he had good support from Benskin and Bill Shipman's younger brother Alan, King was not needed so much, and indeed did not bowl at all in some matches in mid-season. *Wisden* considers Astill, King and the amateur Aubrey Sharp, who appeared in less than half the games, as the stars in a season which saw Leicestershire moving up to eleventh place and winning a record ten matches. In one issue of this, its inaugural year, *The Cricketer* chose to honour King with its front-page feature, replete with photograph of him posing as bowler.

The county's great match of the season, and one written up extensively in the newspapers and *The Cricketer*, was that against the powerful and exciting Australian side, the eagerly awaited opening match of the tour. Crowds packed the ground to witness what proved a one-sided match on an alarmingly fast pitch made seemingly even more fearsome by the contrasting actions of the opening bowlers J.M.Gregory and E.A.McDonald, whose speed challenged the reactions of even young men. Never before and never after did King receive so many plaudits for so few runs as he did in his innings. Batting at No.3, but facing the second ball of the match from Gregory, he was immediately hit 'a rather severe blow on the chest' from a short-pitched ball.[39] Though battered and severely bruised all over his body, he never flinched at the onslaught but kept his body in line, played straight and even, with Mounteney, took the fight to the foe, the partnership reaching 50 in under 40 minutes and ultimately 60, when McDonald (eight for

Coachbuilders' craftsmanship on display in the Aylestone Road car park during the Australian match of 1921.

---

39 As daughter Margaret remembered, 'That night when father came home he was bruised right up to here and you could see, and this is no exaggeration, you could see every stitch of the cricket ball, but after being hit he got 33 runs'.

41) had him caught at the wicket for 29. No wonder that he was too injured to take any further part in the match.

Just over two weeks later on the same ground he scored his first post-war century, 127, against Surrey, doubtless finding Hitch and Co light relief in a five-hour defensive display. This was in a losing cause, but in the very next match, after Leicestershire had conceded 479 for nine to Sussex and only just saved the follow-on, King's three for 40 helped his county keep the target of victory within reasonable bounds and his unbeaten 110 brought about an unlikely victory by seven wickets with but a single ball to spare. *Wisden* called the victory 'astonishing' and further remarked that 'Nothing more sensational was seen during the season'. At Old Trafford in June King hit hard to score 125 not out, and when Leicestershire appeared to have quite thrown away the advantage of leading by 81 on the first innings by stumbling to 37 for five, his 87 in two and a half hours enabled Astill to complete a rare victory over these opponents despite Hallows carrying his bat for 110. As for King, he thus narrowly failed to score for a third time two centuries in a match, which would have been a remarkable performance for one his age, especially against such redoubtable foes, but he was indubitably too good a team-man to let that sully his happiness. A good all-round performance of six wickets and 91 runs in the final home match of the season against Glamorgan confirmed his continuing worth. But in the annals of Leicestershire cricket the more significant match was the corresponding one at Swansea. The Welsh county had won its inaugural match, against Sussex at Cardiff, and now faced Leicestershire. After King's 61 had helped the visitors to a lead of 143, they were humbled for a woeful 70 in the second innings, but eked out a victory by 20 runs thanks to King's five wickets, which included the last man, Harry Creber, the professional and groundsman of the local club, who succumbed lbw. Thus Leicestershire became the first county to defeat the sixteen others that had been admitted to the Championship since it was placed on a regular footing in 1890, a record that it continued by being the first county to defeat Durham upon its accession in 1992. For King personally it meant that he had been a member of his county's team in its inaugural Championship victory over no fewer than eleven counties: Derbyshire, Essex, Glamorgan, Gloucestershire, Lancashire, Middlesex, Northamptonshire, Somerset, Sussex, Worcestershire and Yorkshire.

Leicestershire's bowling, from 1922 onwards for over a decade, was largely in the hands of Astill and Geary. King, in this first year, found it hard to obtain much bite even on his favourite soft pitches and took a mere but not particularly expensive 22 wickets, his best return being five for 72 at Trent Bridge when he had a surprisingly long spell of 25 overs. In many matches he was not called upon at all to turn over his arm. Notwithstanding, he appeared in all 26 Championship matches as a batsman, had the largest aggregate and scored the highest score of the season for Leicestershire, who finished a disappointing fourteenth.

That highest score, 132 at Southampton twenty-one years after his first century on the ground, brought forth an eulogy from the *Leicester Mercury's* reporter: 'The Lutterworth professional, who, during his four and a half hours at the wicket, had occasionally varied his superb defence with flashes of brilliant work on the off-side, and by powerful hitting to the leg, played a really magnificent innings, which once more proved what an extraordinary veteran he is . . . his sustained power after the lapse of so many years entitles him to a unique place amongst present-day cricketers'. His other century came at home against Kent in a high-scoring drawn game. Following his side's second-highest score of 58 in the first innings he made a 'masterly' and chanceless 103 against, among others, the great Frank Woolley and 'Tich' Freeman. This was the last time that his century came in his side's second innings, but his ratio of 15 such centuries to 19 in the first innings is quite unusual, and indicates how often, though not in this particular instance, he was the anchor when the pitch was deteriorating and his side was pressing for victory or attempting to stave off defeat. On several other occasions this year he made Leicestershire's highest innings, most notably a doughty unbeaten 87 against Lancashire at Leicester in a match that was lost by two runs to a run-out, 79 at Gravesend when the next highest was 26 as Woolley, 'who was making the ball do weird things', and Freeman dominated, and 40 when there were only two other scores in double figures but four ducks in the second innings of Astill's benefit match against Sussex. Although in that innings his legs betrayed him and he was run out, he yet managed, again at Leicester, to reach an exhilarating 51 in only a shade over the hour against Northamptonshire.

1923 was much like 1922 – again King had the highest Championship aggregate (and this time the highest average of regular players), again the highest score, again one five-wicket analysis, and but a single wicket more at a similar average, and again Leicestershire finished fourteenth. Despite his age, and occasional neuralgia, he was included in the touring party for Leicestershire's tour of the far north of Scotland when the Agricultural Society held its show on the Aylestone Road ground in July.

For the last time in his career his bowling played an important rôle in a match: on 17 August his five wickets for 31 runs in 52 balls hustled Glamorgan to a defeat at Leicester made possible, with major contributions from Taylor and Astill, by his own 59 after the county had suffered a deficit in the first innings. One wicket, however, he probably subsequently regretted, even though it was that of a man destined to make a great name for himself, the redoubtable R.E.S.Wyatt, for it was this that against Warwickshire at Edgbaston deprived Ewart Astill of a full set of ten, a feat that had never been accomplished for the county up to that time and only once, by George Geary in 1929, since.

He took a long time to get going in batting, his average, finally 32.17 in the Championship, standing at 7.70 after his first ten innings during which he suffered a badly cut finger against Surrey; but his 60 against Sussex in early June was 'evidence that his bat is still a power in the land'. Against Gloucestershire at Leicester he was top scorer in both innings with 68 and 48, as at Maidstone with 40 and an unbeaten 71; and again at Leicester he showed that his skill could yet triumph over failing reactions when he with 36 and Astill with 27 alone withstood the fearsome combination of Robinson, Macaulay, Roy Kilner and Rhodes in a first-innings total of 129 boosted by extras. It was for another match, however, that his fame was bruited far and wide.

Hampshire had scored 252 on the Saturday at Aylestone Road, and Leicestershire had lost two cheap wickets when King joined Astill on Monday, 2 July. Both scored centuries, the latter departing for 106 after they had added 215; but King continued against bowlers no less than Kennedy and Newman who were to take 295 Championship wickets between them that summer. He batted throughout the day, bar a brief delay for bad light and rain. Next morning he still had the energy to be stumped; but by that time he had mulcted Hampshire to the amount of 205 runs, an innings containing 28 fours and but a single observable error. There were eleven other double-centuries during the season, but none other scored on 52-year-old legs.[40]

The home match against Kent was awarded him for a second benefit in recognition of his many years of loyal service. This time he was able to play and was rewarded with an unexpected victory, only the second for the county over these strong opponents in 25 attempts (with as many as 21 defeats). King himself had much to do with this triumph, making the second-highest score of 73 in the first innings, and then, when Benskin and Astill had skittled out the 'Hoppers' to give a lead of 172, top-scoring with 48 out of a poor total of 145 to ensure that the visitors' final task was just a little too hard. Showery weather unfortunately so discouraged spectators that he made an actual loss on the match of £57 8s 8d, which made even more tasteless a cartoon by R.B.Davis in the local *Sports Mercury* the day after the conclusion of the match showing him with a fat cigar at a table loaded with bags and the unpunctuated doggerel verses:

> The King was in his Counting House
> Counting hoards of money
> He handled it with loving care
> And counts the prospect sunny.

Nonetheless, contributions from other sources gave him a final profit of £388 16s 1d, no mean sum at the time for a professional from an unfashionable county.

In 1924 he took his final three wickets. His last at home, to a catch by Geary, was that of J.M.Hutchinson, a nice coincidence for, though the Derbyshire batsman could not rival King's years at Leicester, he was, historians believe, to create his own record of longevity as a first-class cricketer by dying in 2000 just two weeks shy of 104. King's last victim, and a second nice coincidence, was another cricketer who like King played past the fiftieth anniversary of his birth, Glamorgan's doughty J.C.Clay, trapped lbw for nought at Swansea at the end of May.

---

[40] He beat the record for longevity set just a few months before by Archie MacLaren. To this day only 'Dave' Nourse has ever scored a double-century in first-class cricket at a greater age, and King's is still the record in English cricket. The full list of quinquagenarians' first-class double-centuries is 219* by A.W.Nourse at 53 years/337 days for Western Province v Natal at Cape Town in 1932/1933; 205 by J.H.King at 52/78 for Leicestershire v Hampshire at Leicester in 1923; 200* by A.C.MacLaren at 51/29 days for MCC v New Zealand XI at Wellington in 1922/1923; 221 by J.B.Hobbs at 50/162 days for Surrey v West Indians at The Oval in 1933; 200 by C.K.Nayudu at 50/142 for Holkar v Baroda at Indore in 1945/1946.

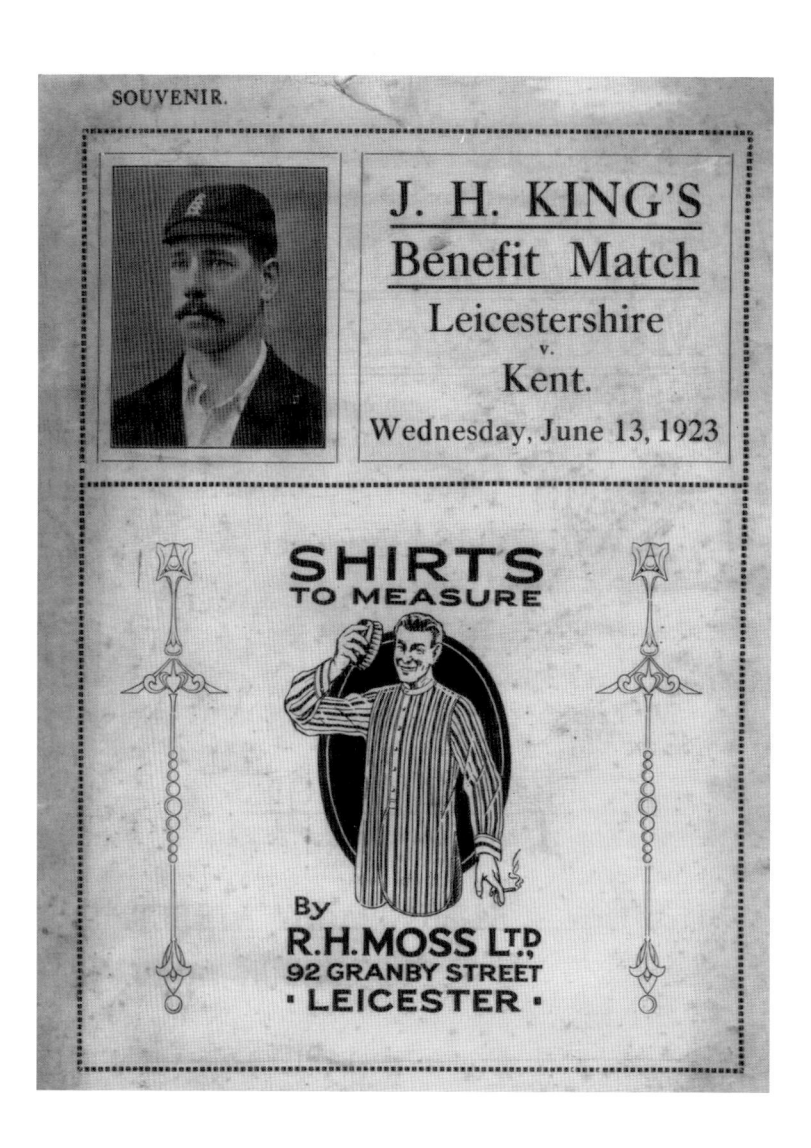

*The brochure of King's second benefit.
The return was worth £15,900 at 2009 prices.*

As a batsman King did his duty by his county, which moved up the table to eleventh, even though the target of 1,000 runs eluded him, perhaps owing to his missing three matches, two at the end of the season resulting from a finger being split by Maurice Tate. His average was a paltry 22.20 in Championship matches, but only two regular players were above him, and then only at 27.57 and 22.97, in a very low-scoring year.[41] His highest innings was 92, achieved twice, and both times as the highest score in the match on either side. The first came at Leicester, when rain prevented a deserved and easy victory against Nottinghamshire, and, in addition to 'defence like a book', he 'revealed much of his old power, with flashing hits on the off-side, and certainty in his strokes to leg'. The second was in Geary's benefit match against Warwickshire, which the beneficiary emphatically ended to give his side an innings victory. King had another good match with 54 and 43* at Leyton and scored a crucial 47 in the victory by a single run over Gloucestershire, while his 10 at Tunbridge Wells was the only score in double figures amid a quite woeful display by his team-mates.

King opened what was to be the last chapter of his playing career with a century at Hove on 2 May 1925, one of only five scored for the county in the whole summer. He thus emulated the feat performed by his erstwhile colleague Sam Coe who also had made the first-class season's opening century, in 1914. It was a fine performance, for the 'pitch [was] on the soft side owing to recent rains' and 'the ball wanted close watching, as the fielding was smart'. Newspapers and *The Cricketer* made much of the fact that this innings was scored by the oldest man still engaged in first-class cricket, and to this day no other cricketer of this age has played regularly in the Championship apart from W.G.Quaife.[42] An old friend – the signature is B.White – from his days at Birkenhead Park enclosed a cutting from the *Liverpool Echo* celebrating the feat 'against such trundlers as the mighty Gilligan and Tate' in a letter expressing his own wildly optimistic hope that it heralded 'still better things'. Although *Wisden* records that he made 114 of

---

41   In the Championship overall, runs were scored in this season at 21.00 per wicket; Leicestershire scored its runs at 16.06 per wicket.
42   The diminutive Quaife played regularly for Warwickshire in 1927 at the age of 55. More than twenty other cricketers have played individual matches in the British Isles at an older age. King's age on the last day of his last match was 54 years and 114 days. For Leicestershire only C.E.de Trafford, who played a single match after a long gap at 56 years and 24 days, has played at a more advanced age.

the 205 runs scored while he was at the wicket, it fails to mention that his score was more than the combined 110 of all his ten colleagues (and only 12 fewer than the 11 men of Sussex achieved), a really remarkable feat for a 54-year-old.[43]

	BATSMEN'S NAMES	HOW OUT	BOWLER	TOTALS
1	Maj G H S Fowke (capt)	LBW	Bowley	46
2	Lord A	Bowled	A E Gilligan	0
3	Berry L G	Bowled	Tate	0
4	King J H	Bowled	Tate	114
5	Astill W E	c. Bowley	Wensley	39
6	Geary G	c. A E Gilligan	Wensley	1
7	Coulson S	LBW	Tate	6
8	Starmer C E	Bowled	Tate	5
9	Sidwell J E	not	out	11
10	Bale J	Bowled	A E Gilligan	1
11	Shipman A	st Cornford	Tate	1

BYES 119, TOTAL EXTRAS 5, TOTAL 229

RUNS AT THE FALL OF EACH WICKET: 1 for 3, 2 for 4, 3 for 108, 4 for 189, 5 for 195, 6 for 209, 7 for 212, 8 for 223, 9 for 224, 10 for 229

Going in at 4 for two, King scored his last first-class century, at Hove in May 1925, facing Maurice Tate at the peak of his powers.

He certainly began the season in marvellous form, for in the very next match, 'looking all over the best bat', he made 70 against Glamorgan at Leicester. The next highest score in the match was Geary's 39 and nobody else reached 20. Opposed to his 70 were 195 from 32 other innings (an average of 6.09: there were also 15 extras). King, on his own, beat each of his opponents' puny efforts of 60 and 36, as Astill and Geary bowled unchanged to bring about an easy victory in only six and a half hours of play. But only once more, with 91 on a fast wicket at Blackheath, when the next highest

---

43   His age was 54 years and 16 days, the highest at the time for a centurion in the Championship. Three years later Willie Quaife scored 115 against Derbyshire on 4 August in his last match for Warwickshire (and only one of the season) at the age of 56 years and 140 days. Since Quaife and W.G.Grace, with three each, are the only players to have scored first-class centuries at a more advanced age, King remains the most elderly left-handed centurion.

score by a colleague in either innings was 33, did he for the last time of so many times shine for his faithful followers like Portia's lamp in the inspissating gloom.

Two weeks after the match against Glamorgan came the crowning accolade from his county: Major Fowke had strained a tendon in his leg and the captaincy for the match at Old Trafford was entrusted to King. Although victory eluded him, the match until the last two hours was hard fought and very evenly balanced, his judgements were sound and he did not disgrace himself with 29 and 21 when neither team managed more than Leicestershire's total of 247 in an innings. The local sports paper commented that it was 'an honour which one was glad to see him enjoy, as a fitting incident in a long and distinguished career'.

His last match was appropriately against Yorkshire on August 5 to 7, appropriately because he played altogether 55 times against Yorkshire, ten more than against any other county. Rain interfered and the match was abandoned when Geary was out after a light-hearted century stand with Astill in the second innings. So King, due to bat next, had to be content with ending his career lbw b Macaulay 11; his consolation, if he needed one, was that he had helped his side to a narrow first-innings lead over its inveterate and formidable foes. His last bowl had been three weeks before, two overs for six runs at Coventry. It was his decision to retire. He missed his county's last six games. If he had played in these and in four earlier ones he would probably have reached 1,000 runs again, for he was only 227 short of that figure; but he had made only 137 in his last ten innings for Leicestershire, interspersed admittedly by his last half-century, a score of 61 (his share of a 150 partnership with C.H.Titchmarsh) in his last representative match, for MCC *v* Oxford University at his beloved Lord's. It was time to go.

Nevertheless, there was still one more personal achievement accomplished this season. In late July he appeared in a friendly two-day game against Durham at Sunderland which has given him today an unique record: he is the sole Leicestershire cricketer to have played for or against all the twenty counties that have taken part in first-class cricket, for he had represented his own county against the other sixteen playing in the 1920s, had appeared in a few matches against London County in the first decade of the twentieth century and had scored a century for MCC in a second-class match against Cambridgeshire in the last year of the nineteenth century.

Wisden's valediction concludes with the summation: 'The most efficient left-handed batsmen ever to play for Leicestershire, and a slow left-arm bowler capable of dismissing any side cheaply on a damaged pitch, King leaves a vacancy very hard to fill'. The last few words hardly apply to his bowling, since he took no wickets in his 20 overs this year, only three for 161 runs the previous year and a mere 45 combined in 1922 and 1923, but his Championship batting average, though seemingly poor at 23.26, yet put him third for the county behind Astill and C.H.Taylor, of whom the latter played but 13 innings. It would have been interesting to hear the discussion at the Leicestershire committee's meeting at the conclusion of the season: how was the decision reached to award him the precise sum of £7 4s 0d out of the £150 available as 'talent money'?

Chapter Eleven
Retirement

During the winter months of his retirement King spent much of his time at the Leicester Liberal Club, keeping up with world news by reading the newspapers there, talking with friends and playing, 'every day' according to his daughter, both bridge and billiards, at which latter game he was no mean adept. In 1920 the club had instituted a handicap competition for a handsome silver trophy, which that year was won by King's colleague Ewart Astill, with whom he often played. Whether after that Astill was too severely handicapped, simply absent abroad or, on account of his clear superiority over other members,[44] he graciously declined to compete, I have not been able to ascertain; but various members won until King, by winning three times (1927, 1932 and 1934), was allowed to keep the trophy, now in the possession of his grand-daughter Judy Cockroft.

Leicester Liberals' billiards cup, won outright by King in 1934.

He also had the opportunity to devote more time to the masons. Like his father before him he had been initiated into the Wiclif Lodge in Lutterworth, in 1907, and subsequently he was elected its Master in 1930. Desirous, however, of progressing through higher grades he joined also, in 1932, the Royal Arch East Goscote Chapter of the York rite at Syston. In 1938 he enjoyed (and surely he did enjoy) the position of Provincial Grand Sword-Bearer for Leicestershire and Rutland, for the performance of whose duties he was accoutred with the implement that warranted his title. More humbly attired he continued also to shoot and fish for the table; and kept fit by doing shoulder-exercises and all the digging in his large garden at home.

---

44   In the winter of 1922/23 Astill reached the third round of the national Amateur Championship.

During the summers, however, beginning in 1926 he was on the first-class umpires' list. His daughter asseverated that he once awarded nine runs on the ground that a fieldsman had deliberately knocked the ball over the boundary after the batsmen had already run five. This incident probably occurred in some friendly match, but it does indicate King's preference for moral over legal justice. In his years on the official list King stood in a total of 170 first-class matches, of which 144 were in the Championship, with most of the other matches between counties and universities, or between counties and touring sides. He was never selected for 'higher' representative fixtures, though he did officiate in two matches at the Scarborough Festival of 1929, alongside David Denton. All his duties were, for him, 'away' matches, because at that time umpires were not permitted to stand in matches involving their previous 'playing' counties.[45] The authorities at Lord's, at any rate, were satisfied with his adherence to the Laws of the game, for he remained on the list for seven years until the conclusion of the 1932 season when, now 61, he retired because of failing health. He was presumably reasonably fit earlier on that year, however, for the county archives reveal that on 30 April he was paid £32 for coaching.

After a gap of one year he is to be found employed from 1934 to 1936 as one of Oxford University's two umpires, standing in 25 first-class matches, all University home fixtures in May and early June.[46] He officiated also in the freshmen's and seniors' trial matches in each of those seasons. How he came to be appointed is readily understood when it is remembered that whereas most umpires were, in those class-conscious days, of the proletariate, King was clearly from a higher social stratum, was indeed a past master of a masonic lodge and, despite the contretemps with Lord Hawke, could always associate by means of a deference allied to a consciousness of his own worth with members of the upper

---

[45] It seems highly likely that King would have conducted himself as an umpire with quiet dignity, a quality unlikely to attract comment: indeed as a freemason, he probably appreciated the ceremonial aspect of cricket. It is odd therefore to find that the only published comment on the style of his umpiring is that by A.E.R.Gilligan suggesting that he was perhaps a little frivolous. Gilligan says in his book *Sussex Cricket* that 'Jack afterwards became a first class umpire, and whenever he gave a batsman out, he would invariably cry, "Chuck her up", that grand cry which is so often heard on village greens. The reason for the cry "Chuck her up" originated years and years ago, when a delighted fieldsman made a wonderful catch and, to show his uncommon pleasure, hurled a ball a prodigious distance into the air.' From all that we know of King, such behaviour seems quite out of character.

[46] Although the universities played first-class matches against the counties, their umpires at that time were not drawn from the Championship list.

classes. His daughter remarked that he 'had the open sesame for invitations by wealthy amateurs such as Lord and Lady Swaythling on whose yacht he used to sail out of Southampton'.[47] In part because of this he had been chosen to officiate in two of the four great social cricketing occasions of the year at Lord's: not the Test or the Gentlemen v Players match but three 'Varsity matches (1928-1930) and four Eton v Harrow matches (1927-1930), usually with the ex-Derbyshire all-rounder Arthur Morton. His demeanour and appearance on such occasions may have reminded some elderly followers of his county of Frankfort Moore's humorous description of umpires in the *Leicester Daily Mercury* of 26 May 1900, that 'in their long linen overalls [they] were the honorary chaplains to the MCC wearing their surplices'.[48] Fittingly King's very last match as a first-class umpire was on 14, 15 and 16 June 1936, when he had the satisfaction of seeing Les Berry, his young colleague during his last two years as a cricketer for Leicestershire, score a century in the drawn game against Oxford University at The Parks. He must still have umpired on occasion in minor matches after that date, since Philip Snow insists that it was in either 1937 or 1938 that he invited him to dine at Christ's when King was umpiring a match at Cambridge. At some point during this period of his life he was also employed to coach the son of the Duke and Duchess of Devonshire at Chatsworth; but he never lost his interest in or involvement with Leicestershire. From time to time he coached, watched when he could and gave advice and judgements when asked. In the last he was honest but tactful, never, for instance, speaking at Aylestone Road as bluntly as he

---

47   His circle of friends and acquaintances was very broad and included members of the upper mercantile class such as Victor Pochin of the family that ran the large hardware business in Leicester. He also, his daughter told me, 'got on very well' with that shrewd, tenacious, principled, and often misunderstood, Wykehamist and Oxonian Douglas Jardine, a man brought up by a family of lawyers in the tenets of the British Raj.

48   If he had lived long enough to hear or read it, he would have had mingled approval and disapprobation of the poem on umpires by his former county colleague and later fellow umpire Alec Skelding, which began

> Portrayed by most cartoonists as a 'Snoozer',
> With red proboscis claiming him a 'Boozer',
> And a mien most dejected,
> As if spinally affected,
> Whom the tossed coin makes an everlasting loser.
> Six hours a day – if there's actual play,
> He stands as in thought, clad in white array;
> Confident, though in purgatory,
> Prepared for all emergency,
> A martyr to the game – but for his pay !

The whole poem of 141 lines was originally entitled 'Duties, Trials and Troubles of County Umpires', but Skelding later adopted Brian Sellers' suggestion of 'The Umpire's Lament'. It may be found in the Leicestershire County Cricket Club Yearbook for 1960, pp 73-75.

did privately to his daughter, who remembered him, for instance, criticizing the decision to give a trial in the first team to the son of Aubrey Temple Sharp, that gifted batsman who sadly for the county chose the professional life of a solicitor rather than that of a cricketer: J.A.T.Sharp, he prognosticated, will 'never play cricket as long as he lives'.[49] King's last active involvement with cricket came during the Second World War, at which time he appears as an umpire in scorecards of more than twenty of his native county's matches.

As for his domestic life in retirement, he was very content until his wife died. 'Father led exactly the life he wanted to; and it was wonderful really, wasn't it? He smoked a pipe and drank little', was the observation to me of his daughter, whose wedding photograph of him with her, on 20 September 1932 at the same church in which he himself had been married, shows him in splendid form. At that time they were still living at Rutland House, but Florence's death at the early age of 53 around 1930[50] left him bereft: 'He was at a loss around the house' apart, presumably, from cooking, being

King with daughter Margaret on her wedding day in 1932.

King with his grand-daughter, Carol, probably in 1940.

---

49 General Sir John Sharp, MC did have other talents, which he exercised on behalf of his country until he died suddenly at the age of 59, in Norway in January, 1977, a death, as all Leicestershire cricket believed, from poison administered by an Eastern bloc agent.
50 I cannot ascertain the exact date.

'hopeless – I never saw father knock a nail in: he couldn't do a thing', in curious contrast with his interest and competence in the garden.

Since he wished, nevertheless, for independence and would not stay beholden to daughter and son-in-law in houses that they had built in Scraptoft or Rothley, he lived on his own at 38 Brinsmead Road in Leicester and, by 1940, at 107 Lothair Road, but eventually, suffering from diabetes, he went to stay with his daughter, by that time a widow, in Denbigh, North Wales. He died in that town, at The Abbey House Nursing Home, on 18 November 1946, seven months after his close friend Knight, and was buried in the graveyard of Lutterworth parish church, to be joined there later by his brother and, in 2004, by his daughter's ashes. At his funeral the Psalm was No.53, 'The fool hath said in his heart, There is no God', and the hymns were 'Abide with me' and 'Lead, kindly light', while Handel's 'I know that my Redeemer liveth' from 'Messiah' and Spohr's 'O rest in the Lord' were played on the organ. His memory was perpetuated in his home town by the naming in about 1950 of a short street, King's Way, joining Woodway Road and Elmhirst Road and continued by Whittle Road, which perpetuates the memory of another famous figure intimately connected with the town. And it is kept vivid in his family by his grand-daughter and great-grandson Timothy, who once as a little boy sent his grandmother a birthday card consisting entirely of King's cricketing statistics.

His family clearly had sporting genes: besides his brother James, his nephew John William, after playing 40 matches for Worcestershire in 1927 and 1928, appeared in eight for his native county in 1929 to become the third member of the family to represent Leicestershire. His grandson, Christopher Wearn, chose another of King's sports, helping his school, Uppingham, win the Michael Farriday Trophy in Canada, shooting for the Combined Cadet Force and internationally for Wales and reaching the shoot-off for a place in the team for the Commonwealth Games.

The best-known sportsman in the family after King himself is, however, great-grandson Timothy Cockroft, son of Margaret's daughter Judy (with sporting, hand-eye co-ordination genes inherited also from his father Richard who played for Devon Dumplings). Timothy was in the first eleven at Wellington College, played for Berkshire Under-19s, was a member of the Old Wellingtonian team that won *The Cricketer* Cup in 1996 and now

Timothy Cockroft, King's great-grandson, is one of the world's leading amateur rackets players.

plays for the Hurlingham club, for which he regularly averages approximately 50 runs an innings. He was also in his school's and Berkshire's Under-19 hockey teams and was captain of the former's squash first five; but it is in rackets that he has really made his name. A member of his school's rackets first pair, he later joined with Toby Sawrey-Cookson to win the Noel Bruce Cup in 1998/99 for the only time in the Old Wellingtonians' history. Together with Mark Hue-Williams he won the national Under-24 Doubles for the four years from 1988 to 1991 and the individual title also in 1991. No fewer than seven times, with four different partners, he has won the Amateur Doubles Championship (1992, 1994, 1996, 1997, 2003, 2005 and 2008), while in 1994, 1995 and 1996 with Willie Boone he won the Open Doubles Championship. He has also three times been in the winning pair in the United States Open Doubles and won both the singles and doubles in the Canadian Amateur Championships of 1997 and 1999. Twice also he has challenged unsuccessfully for the World Doubles Championship, in 1996 with Willie Boone and in 2005 with Guy Smith-Bingham. His sister Georgina, a quondam off-break bowler in the nets at home with her father and brother, was captain of

Leeds University ladies' hockey team and still plays league hockey of a high standard with Wimbledon.

Meanwhile their great-grandfather lies with his brother in the churchyard at Lutterworth. The tombstone, erected by Judy and her husband in 2003, reads simply:

JOHN HERBERT
KING
1871 – 1946
LEICESTERSHIRE
AND ENGLAND CRICKETER
AND HIS BROTHER
JAMES KING
1869 – 1948

The Simonidean restraint of the inscription is reminiscent of that of the Grace Gates at Lord's, scene of King's most famous innings.

Chapter Twelve
Albert Knight's Appreciation

Albert Edward Knight, King's long-time colleague and close friend, was not only a Test player, but also author of the only book on cricket that C.B.Fry is reputed to have envied. It was commonly believed, however, that its style and command of English were beyond the compass of a mere professional sportsman. The tone is set by the opening sentence: 'Antecedent to the beginning of the eighteenth century, cricket history is, in the main, a record of conjecture, the sifting of inferences previously hazarded, the weighing of evidences largely hypothetical'. Critics, contemporary and recent (even so distinguished a cricket writer as J.M.Kilburn) seem to have ignored, or been unaware of, the fact that Knight had attended the Wyggeston School in Leicester (to-day eviscerated and magniloquently styled Wyggeston and Queen Elizabeth I Sixth-Form College). Here he had learned Latin, ever a fine training for mastery of English grammar and vocabulary, and had become sufficiently enamoured of it to make classical allusions during a match.[51] He was, moreover, a Methodist lay preacher.[52] The appreciation of King that he wrote for his friend's benefit brochure in 1923 is stylistically of a

Albert Knight was one of King's Leicestershire colleagues for seventeen seasons.

---

51   He was in general a cultured man, well-versed in English (and some foreign) literature and knowledgeable in music, who used to attend lectures at the Literary and Philosophical Society in Leicester ('People who don't attend them say they are abominably "dry"; people who do presumably differ'). The fact, however, that he was once employed in the lowly trade of 'shoe clicker' suggests that he had had to leave school at a comparatively early age and was in consequence to a considerable extent self-taught.

52   His piety was even more evident than his devotion to the Classics. It is famously told of him that once on holding a steepling hit in the outfield he sank to his knee (some accounts less probably record knees). Upon enquiry over his well-being by his captain, he replied that he 'was thanking' his 'Maker'.

piece with the book, thus giving the lie to doubts of the latter's authorship (as do his columns in the *Leicester Daily Mercury* of 1904[53]), and deserves to be better known. It is quoted here, in its entirety, for the extra light it sheds on its subject. Probably because he was a batsman (and splendid cover-point) Knight does, however, almost completely overlook King's abilities as a bowler.

Some Memories of J.H.King

It is some thirty years ago since King and I first played together in a kind of county trial against Uppingham Rovers on the old ground at Aylestone. The lithe and slender figure of those days has thickened and the astonishing quickness in the field has passed. The great love of the game, the superb physique and stamina, the technical skill, the shrewd assiduity – these have stayed with him and contributed to a supremacy more prolonged than any hitherto known in Leicestershire cricket.

It is perhaps one of the advantages of age – if it may be said to have advantages – that it looks as from some lone observatory above the mists and worries always around the present, to see the figures of the past serene and beautiful as the stars. One hears again the pavilion bell that broke up all discussion and quickened lingering feet from out the rough-timbered fastness that hid all sight of the Aylestone field. There were giants then – although many are but voiceless shadows now. What a fine bowler was Pougher; and has poor Bill Tomlin's late cut ever been surpassed or his rich unconscious humour ? And as a wicket-keeper purely, have there been many better than Whiteside?

The correctness of King's early style, his keen watchfulness of the ball right on to the bat impressed Arnold Rylott, the genial and aged Leicester bowler, who always spoke of him as pre-eminently a batsman rather than the bowler whom others foreshadowed. In later years the watchfulness may not have been so marked, but his superb driving through the covers, the splendid freeness of his arm swing and the quick swiftness of his flashing cut had qualities belonging to the permanent and the real no less than to the transient. I vividly remember a cut

---

53 It cannot now be ascertained why he did not have a contract in 1905, but it may be conjectured without great risk of inviting derision that the editor or proprietor found his English to be too high-flown and at times sesquipedalian for a provincial newspaper's readership. Further examples of his prose may be found on pages 21, 43 and 53.

for six – not run out – on the present County Ground from a Surrey bowler. The wickets were pitched rather near to the tea pavilion side, and the cut landed on the white rail – the only over-the-boundary cut I ever remember to have seen.

Most habitués of the Leicester ground must think of King as stationed in the slips, where his telescopic arms and sure fingers do not let much escape him. In these early days he was as dashing and brilliant a fieldsman, as quick a racer to the boundary as one has seen. Round about the middle nineties, at Sheffield, *v* Yorkshire, King gave a display of fielding which he never repeated. I cannot think it was ever surpassed even by Tom Jayes, the most superb and active fieldsman who ever wore the Leicester colours. King, in this game, was at cover-point, and he stopped the ball with his head, hands, feet, and every part of his anatomy. The ball could not pass him. Yorkshire then, as nearly always, were a great fielding side, and the Sheffield crowd is very critical. King did not come in to bat until No.10 or No.11, but he then received an ovation, in appreciation of his work in the field, which many subsequent triumphs of his, both with bat and ball, cannot but recall. One incident in this particular game illustrates the shrewd imperturbability so characteristic. The ball was hit down the long slope to the Press-box, Jack after it. As he reached it, one doubted whether it would roll to the cinder boundary or not. The Yorkshiremen had already run four or five for the stroke. With extended arms, like a maid about to dive and half afraid to do so, King watched the expiring trickle of the ball. Whether it did touch the track for four or was ultimately returned when six had been run, I forget now. Mr Hillyard, the tennis player, was the bowler, a gentleman apt to get irritated when punished, and he could not understand the wisdom of King's hesitancy. His comment, like that of Bret Hart[e]'s Californian, was "frequent and painful and free".

Rather curiously, when one thinks of that other fine veteran whom Time in its "race of hours" seems not to have wearied, Sam Coe, the memory of his early fielding predominates. As a colt – how well the forgotten term illustrates the frisky, fractious, indiarubber-ball sort of youth Sam was – he was extraordinarily quick in picking up and returning the ball.

Dr Grace, in his later years, professed to believe that King and I were always arguing at the wicket over the validity of runs short or otherwise. I confess that King was not always ready to respond to the call as one would have desired. I suppose he felt, as a boy assured me only to-day, that he would have responded all right, but "I should surely have been out!" One match at Nottingham in the early 1900's I shall never forget. On the last day of the match, Leicester were some five or six hundred runs behind and had an innings defeat to avert. With an innings of 150 or so King stayed the whole day and determinedly saved us. Harry Whitehead had accompanied King to the wicket, and became so irritated at King's refusal to run the long runs to deep extra cover that he proceeded to the far wicket to drag him out of his crease. How futile the effort or the appeal to the Sphinx! Poor Harry at last galloped back and even then nearly got home so long was the run. How frequently did he turn in his disgust to look at the mute column of his partner; how concentrated looked his malevolence; how long a time he was getting to the pavilion! I followed Whitehead and was as annoyed as later one was amused by the magnificent endowments, Mercury-like in quality, King gave to those Notts fieldsmen – even to Tom Wass. But the result! A magnificent draw entirely due to the skill and the character of King.[54]

One calls to mind so many great performances of King, both for the county and at Lord's, that one would almost write a history of the county during this past 25 or 30 years were one now to amplify them. A sustained spell of great bowling that enabled us to win one of our rare victories over Yorkshire at Leicester, and a dour innings on a fiery wicket against Worcester at Leicester – turning prospective defeat into a brilliant victory – stand out for me amongst so many invaluable efforts for his side. It is a great pleasure to think of these, a still greater pleasure to recall one's long friendship with so fine a man. At long last one supposes even this superb physique will tire and turn into the lane that leads to the pavilion and to rest. No one player has done so much as he to feed the high tradition of Leicestershire cricket. Let us hope others may as happily follow him.

---

54   In the 1903 match at Trent Bridge, to which Knight refers, King scored 127, being engaged in a partnership of 241 in four hours and three quarters with Knight himself, who finished with 144 not out.

Chapter Thirteen
His Place in Leicestershire's Annals

John King's final figures, in 502 matches for his native county, were: in batting 896 innings, 64 times not out, 22,618 runs, a highest score of 227* and an average of 27.19, with 32 centuries and 115 fifties; in bowling he took 1,100 wickets for 27,780 runs at an average of 25.25 with a best return of eight for 17, dismissing five or more batsmen in an innings 64 times and ten or more in a match ten times; and in fielding, although away from the wicket much in his early days, he held 308 catches. He is the only Leicestershire player to have participated in matches against all the other 19 counties to have played first-class matches, since, in addition to representing his county in first-class matches against both London County and the other 16 members of the Championship during his career, he played in non-first-class matches once for MCC against Cambridgeshire, scoring a century, and once for Leicestershire against Durham.

Without possibility of argument he is the finest and most prolific left-handed all-rounder that was ever produced by or represented Leicestershire. The Australian Jack Walsh may have been a better, and certainly was a more exciting, bowler, but his batting, though often extremely entertaining, cannot be compared with that of his predecessor; the Surrey-born Tony Lock, unarguably a superior bowler, was vastly inferior as a batsman (right-handed, of course) and played for Leicestershire for only three seasons.

At the time of his retirement King had played more matches and scored more runs, and had more thousand-run seasons in all first-class matches (14: he narrowly missed the target on two further occasions by 9 and 36 runs) than any other player for the county: and was overtaken by Ewart Astill for most wickets only after his final dismissal and when he had but three matches to play and two overs to bowl. He was second to C.J.B.Wood for most centuries (32) and fifties (115 excluding centuries), second to Astill for 5-wicket innings (64) and 10-wicket matches (10), second equal after Wood for thousand-run seasons (10) and to Whitehead for catches held in the field (309). Even to-day, over eighty years later, he is second for 1,000- run seasons in all matches (after Berry), and third in Leicestershire matches only for matches played (after Astill and Berry) and runs scored (after Berry and Hallam), fourth for fifties (after Berry, Wood and Hallam), fifth for wickets taken (after Astill, Geary, Spencer and Walsh), 5-wicket innings and 10-wicket matches (both after Astill, Geary, Walsh and Haydon Smith), sixth equal for centuries (after Berry, Davison, Armstrong, Whitaker and Wood) and seventh for catches (after Hallam, Whitehead, Astill, Spencer, Geary and Steele). Of the players above him in one or more category Wood, Berry, Walsh, Davison, Whitaker and Steele were not Leicestershire-born.

His pre-eminence as a left-hander is illustrated by the fact that he is still first in every category mentioned except for wickets taken, wherein the Australian Jack Walsh surpasses him by a mere 27 (but took fewer wickets in all first-class matches). John Steele held more catches, but while bowling left he batted right. Furthermore, given the drastic reduction in first-class matches, it is highly unlikely that in the future his position will drop in any of these categories apart possibly from centuries.

Against individual counties he has scored the most runs for Leicestershire against Hampshire and Surrey and by a left-hander also against Derbyshire, Kent, Northamptonshire, Nottinghamshire, Sussex, Worcestershire and Yorkshire; the highest individual score against Hampshire and by a left-hander also against Derbyshire, Worcestershire and Yorkshire. For most wickets he is usually behind the prolific Astill and Geary and sometimes Spencer, but as a left-hander, despite the large totals by Walsh, he has taken most of any bowler for Leicestershire against Derbyshire, Hampshire Lancashire, Nottinghamshire, Surrey, Warwickshire and Yorkshire. His innings analyses against Derbyshire, Kent, Somerset and Yorkshire are still statistically the best by a left-hander.

He was also the first Leicestershire player to play in a home Test (and the third over-all after Pougher and Knight); the first to perform the hat-trick in first-class cricket (Arnall-Thompson and Pougher had done so in second-class days), the first to perform this feat twice, the first to perform the season's double (albeit with the help of some runs in non-County matches); the second (after Knight the previous year) to score a century in the Gentlemen *v* Players match and the only one ever to score two (in the same match) for the Players. (Charles Palmer scored two, in different matches, for the Gentlemen). He is the oldest player to play regularly (at 54); the oldest to score 1,000 runs in a season (at 52); the oldest to score a century (at 54); the oldest to score a double century (at 52); the oldest to take 100 wickets in a season (at 49); the oldest to take five wickets in an innings (at 52); the oldest to take ten wickets in a match (at 49); and the oldest to perform the hat-trick (at 49). Moreover no Leicestershire bowler has ever taken seven wickets in fewer than his 20 balls against Yorkshire. On a less happy note he is also the only batsman for the county ever to have been dismissed 'hitting the ball twice'.

In all the 26 years in which King played for Leicestershire (in odd matches only in 1895, 1897 and 1898 and then regularly from 1899 to 1925 with the exception of 1910, when through injury he played in only two Championship matches, and the four years of war), his county finished in the top half of the competition only twice (seventh in 1904 and fifth in 1905) and in the bottom four no fewer than 17 times, of which it was equal last three times and last-but-one on a further four occasions. The strict rules of qualification and the very limited financial resources of a small and not particularly rich county had the inescapable consequence of a generally weak team. The chances of victory against one of the 'Big Six' counties were always slim. Indeed in the 51 matches against Yorkshire during these years Leicestershire won only two, of the 48 against Surrey again only two, and of the 52 against Lancashire but four, while against Kent there was not even the consolation of a handful of drawn games for out of 30[55] as many as 26 were lost with only two won.

In such circumstances the Leicestershire players (and the same is, of course, true for all the weaker counties) knew that success in the Championship was a mirage at best. It is clear from newspaper reports that paid players often took the field with a defeatist attitude, bowling in dispirited manner against the likes of Hobbs on a 'shirt-front' at the Oval or Fry and 'Ranji' on a sun-baked pitch at Hove, and batting nervously, ever anxious to return to the pavilion unharmed, against the likes of Kortright on a bumpy pitch

---

55   Leicestershire did not play Kent until 1906.

at Leyton or Hirst on a sticky wicket at Bramall Lane.[56] Nowhere, however, to my knowledge is there the slightest suggestion that King did not strive with nerve and sinew to do his utmost however unpromising (and so often it was far more than this) was the situation for his side. Throughout his career there are only four instances of him being recorded as 'retired hurt' on the scorecard, and rarely did an injury keep him out of the game for long.

Mention is common of the fact that he was likely to have won more representative honours if he had played for a county that commanded greater space in the national and metropolitan press, and we may add that his figures would have been more impressive, and consequently his claims more compelling, had he played for a stronger county. Yet again there seems to be no evidence that he expressed or felt any regret that he was tied to a weak county. Early in his career when he was at Birkenhead he was urged to stay in Lancashire, where, it was pointed out, he would have had the chance to qualify for the county team by residence, but he returned to Leicester for, as his daughter said, 'Father wanted to come home'.[57]

The *Leicester Daily Mercury* gives the best, but not the only, evidence of how he was regarded by his county's supporters.

Although he was county-born and county-bred, King was a hardly a local 'lad' when he first started to play for Leicestershire. He made his début in four matches at the age of 24 and when he appeared next (and then only fleetingly) two years later he was already in his second year as a professional with Birkenhead Park. He played with no regularity for his county until he was 28 and had little success before he was 29. The crowds could not, then, take him to heart in a kind of proprietorial and fatherly manner as they could a teenager whom they had followed from his first steps in the Championship (and perhaps even earlier in Club and Ground games). He was no Ewart Astill who was known to keen followers of cricket in Leicester before he first played for the county in a single match at the tender age of 18 and then delighted them with

---

[56] Genuine amateurs (unlike those who could play as amateurs only because their counties gave them non-playing paid employment) were more inclined to play for their personal delight in pitting their courage, wits and technique against the game's most skilled practitioners and gaining glory for combat with a Hobbs or Rhodes.

[57] They must have talked about this, for it happened many years before Margaret was born. It must be admitted, however, that King surely realized that his chances were vastly greater of gaining a regular place in the Leicestershire than in the Lancashire team.

his prowess as he topped the county averages the following year with 80 wickets at only 17.03; and, again unlike Astill, King did not preserve his boyish looks.

In the Edwardian age, as he at last began to fulfill his potential, prove his worth as an all-rounder and perform so valorously on so many occasions, King came to be at first respected and then increasingly admired. His batting did not excite in quite the same way as did that of 'Noisy' de Trafford or 'Very Fast Scoring' Crawford with flamboyant sixes, and, despite often being forceful and free-flowing, it was too correct to encourage spectators to chuckle at mishaps so like their own as did the more rustic strokeplay of Sammy Coe;[58] but, like that of the obdurate warrior 'Cis' Wood, it called forth a wonderment, perhaps even a reverence, and from the time of his two centuries for the Players, when he was lauded on the national stage, supporters took pride in 'our Jack'. His bowling similarly did not excite with the high-speed scatter of stumps like that of Woodcock or Skelding or with the extravagant spin like that later of Jack Walsh[59] which resulted in spectators' hilarity at the discomfiture of bemused batsman and a perplexed wicket-keeper who found that he was, as it were, 'picking a tablet of soap out of the bath';[60] but, again, King was respected and esteemed.

After the Great War older spectators, their active days behind them, admired his achievements of which they were so little capable themselves, and their younger brethren were in awe at what 'an old man' could achieve. They may sometimes have chuckled at his rheumatical scampering to make his ground, but it was a chuckle entirely without malice as at a favourite 'grandpa'. Now at last we can say that supporters felt love for King, but it was a love not to be displayed in any effusive manner – he was too dignified a man for that.

---

58   As Neville Cardus wrote, 'See an innings by Coe . . . and you ought not to be long in guessing from the smack of rotund nature about it that he has passed the main portion of his days in the sun on a field with rustic benches running intimately round'.
59   Jack Fingleton remembered even Bradman playing 'for an off-break and miss[ing] the ball by a good two feet as it spun the other way . . . I had never before seen Bradman so completely beaten'. But Bradman merely commented (in a private letter) that Walsh, although he 'bowled a really good "wrong-un"' . . . 'got a lot of stick for little reward' in that match and 'like all spinners . . . tended to be erratic and had difficulty in controlling length and direction'.
60   Ray Julian in a private letter.

*John Herbert and James King,
cricketing brothers,
are buried in St Mary's Church, Lutterworth.*

Acknowledgements

My sincere thanks are due to the late Margaret Wearn for telling me so much about her father; Richard and Judy Cockroft for further familial information; Philip Snow for answering so many questions and for writing the foreword; Michael Turner, first for encouraging me to believe that I was capable of writing a biography of a Leicestershire cricketer, and recently for commenting sapiently on the chapter 'Technique and Style'; Richard Holdridge for supplying information on Lutterworth Grammar School and reading, correcting and supplementing a late draft; Dennis Lambert for coming to my aid when needed; Chris Elston, Peter Pickup and Tony McCarron for information on King's sojourns in Birkenhead, Eccleshill and Western Province respectively; Adam Sweeting at Lord's for help with research into the details of King's minor matches for MCC; Diane Clements of the Library and Museum of Freemasonry for information about King's career in the craft; and Philip Bailey for his assistance on a variety of statistical points. The staff of the British Library's newspaper library at Colindale kindly gave me every assistance as I spent two week perusing local newspapers in its keeping. I am grateful to David Smith, Chief Executive of Leicestershire County Cricket Club, for consent to reproduce papers in the club's possession. David Jeater has been an ideal editor, correcting errors, unearthing supplementary information and tolerating my many caprices.

For photographs, I am indebted to the archivists at Leicestershire County Cricket Club, Sylvia Michael and Richard Holdridge; Adam Goodwin for having the county scorebooks scanned at the Leicester, Leicestershire and Rutland Record Office; the late Margaret Wearn for loans and gifts; Richard Cockroft for taking photographs at my request; Roger Mann for contributing photographs from his own collection; and Allan Noon for photographing other items. The photographs of Lutterworth church and the grave are my own. Of the items illustrated King's bat, silk scorecard and billiards trophy are in the Cockrofts' possession, his waist-coat buttons, the congratulatory telegram sent to him and his letter to S.C.Packer in mine.

Acknowledgments

May I thank, too, Peter Griffiths for his typesetting and other contributions to the production of the book, Zahra Ridge for her cover design, and Gerald Hudd and John Ward for their proofreading?

Bibliography

The following printed materials have been used to differing extents:

Ambrose, D., *Liverpool and District Cricketers: 1882-1947*, ACS Publications, 2002

Bailey, P.J., Thorn, P.R. and Wynne-Thomas, P., *Who's Who of Cricketers* (Revised Edition), Hamlyn in association with ACS, London, 1993

Beldam, G.W. and Fry, C.B., *Great Batsmen: their methods at a Glance*, MacMillan, London, 1905

Beldam, G.W. and Fry, C.B., *Great Bowlers and Fielders: their methods at a Glance*, MacMillan, London, 1907

Bradford Daily Argus

Brooke, R.W., *The Cricketer Book of Cricket Milestones*, Century Benham for Marks and Spencer, London, 1987

Brooke, R.W., *A History of The County Cricket Championship*, Guinness Publishing, Enfield, 1991

Cardus, N., *Days in the Sun: a Cricketer's Journal*, Grant Richards, London, 1924

Duckworth, L.H., *S.F.Barnes: Master Bowler*, Hutchinson and The Cricketer, London, 1967

Dyson, A.H., *Family History of the Coles of Lutterworth, 1641-1911* (This is a seven-page booklet compiled in 1911 by the honorary secretary of the Lutterworth Literary Institute and presumably privately printed.)

Easdale, R., *England's One Test Wonders*, Parapress, Guildford, 1999

Elston, C.W., *Birkenhead Park Cricket Club 1846-1996*, Eaton Press, Wirral, 1997

Fingleton, J.H., *Brightly Fades the Don*, Collins, London, 1949

Fry, C.B., *Cricket (Batsmanship)*, Nash, London, 1912

Fry, C.B., *Life Worth Living*, Eyre and Spottiswoode, London, 1939

Gibson, A., 'A.E.Knight, 1873-1946', *Journal of the Cricket Society*, 5(2), 1971, pp 40-42

Gilligan, A.E.R., *Sussex Cricket*, Chapman and Hall, London, 1933

Haigh, G., *The Big Ship: Warwick Armstrong and the Making of Modern Cricket*, Text Publishing Company, Australia, 2001

Haygarth, A. and Ashley-Cooper, F.S., *MCC Cricket Scores and Biographies: Volume XV*, Longmans and Co., London, 1925

(Hodgson, R.L.), *Cricket Memories by a Country Vicar*, Methuen, London, 1930

Irving, G., *Lutterworth Grammar School Anniversary Book*, [The School], Lutterworth, 1956

Jeater, D.A., 'County Cricket Grounds and their Geology', *The Cricket Statistician,* 139, 2007, pp 29-35

Knight, A.E., *The Complete Cricketer*, Methuen, London, 1906

Lambert, D.A., *The History of Leicestershire County Cricket Club*, Christopher Helm, London, 1992

Lambert, D.A., *Leicestershire County Cricket Club: First-Class Records 1894-1996*, Limlow Books, 1997

Leicester Daily Mercury (later *Leicester Mercury*)

Lester, J.A. (ed.), *A Century of Philadelphia Cricket*, University of Pennsylvania, Philadelphia, 1951

Leveson Gower, H.D.G., *Off and On the Field*, Stanley Paul, London, 1953

Littlewood, A.R., 'John Herbert King 1871-1946: the Nestor of Leicestershire', *The Canadian Cricketer* 22.1, 1994, pp 40-41

Major, J., *More than a Game: the Story of Cricket's Early Years*, Harper, London, 2007

Nichols, J., *History and Antiquities of the County of Leicester*, Nichols, London, 1795-1811 (Eight volumes)

Noble, M.A., *The Game's the Thing*, Cassell, London, 1926

Payne, S., *A History of Lutterworth Cricket Club 1789 to 1989*, [The Club], Lutterworth, 1989

Percival, A.R., *Cheshire Cricketers: 1822-1996*, ACS, Nottingham, 1997

Pullin, A.W. ('Old Ebor'), *Talks with Old Yorkshire Cricketers* (Second Edition), The Yorkshire Post, Leeds, 1898

Ranjitsinhji, K.S., *The Jubilee Book of Cricket*, Blackwood, Edinburgh and London, 1897

Robertson-Glasgow, R.C., *46 Not Out*, Hollis and Carter, London, 1948

Root, C.F., *A Cricket Pro's Lot*, Edward Arnold, London, 1937

Snow, E.E., *Cricket Grounds of Leicestershire*, Association of Cricket Statisticians, Haughton Mill, n.d.

Snow, E.E., *A History of Leicestershire Cricket*, Edgar Backus, Leicester, 1949

Snow, P.A., *The Years of Hope: Cambridge, Colonial Administration in the South Seas and Cricket*, Radcliffe Press, London and New York, 1997

Sports Mercury (Leicester)

Synge, A., *Sins of Omission: the Story of The Test Selectors 1899-1990*, Pelham Books, London, 1990

Thomson, A.A., *Odd Men In: a Gallery of Cricket Eccentrics*, Pavilion Library, London, 1958

Thomson, A.A., *Cricket: the Golden Ages*, Stanley Paul, London, 1961

Warner, P.F., *Lord's 1787-1945*, Harrap, London, 1946

Wisden's Cricketers' Almanack

The South African newspaper from which quotations are made is probably *The South African News*, but the cuttings lent by Margaret Wearn do not include its title. Newspapers from which other quotations have been made are mentioned in their proper place.

Use has been made also of the websites cricketarchive.com, measuringworth.com and nationaltrustnames.org.uk

Appendix One

Some Statistics

Test cricket

King played in one Test match, for England v Australia at Lord's in 1909. He scored 64 runs in two completed innings and took one wicket for 99 runs in 27 overs, five of which were maidens. He took no catches in the match. A full scorecard of this match is given at Appendix Two.

First-Class cricket: Batting and Fielding

	M	I	NO	R	HS	Ave	100	50	Ct
1895	4	8	2	17	12*	2.83	-	-	2
1897	5	10	0	169	56	16.90	-	1	1
1898	6	11	1	242	77	24.20	-	2	2
1899	20	35	2	537	65	16.27	-	1	7
1900	24	42	3	991	121	25.41	1	6	20
1901	27	49	5	1630	143	37.04	4	9	23
1902	26	47	5	1200	130	28.57	2	4	13
1903	25	44	3	1209	167	29.48	2	9	15
1904	30	51	4	1788	186	38.04	5	9	21
1905	25	40	4	964	95	26.77	0	6	11
1906	26	49	4	1159	126*	25.75	2	4	11
1907	21	40	3	669	80*	18.08	-	3	17
1908	27	45	1	1204	142	27.36	1	11	16
1909	28	48	3	1347	90	29.93	-	11	20
1910	2	4	0	146	60	36.50	-	1	1
1911	25	47	6	1187	118	28.95	3	2	15
1912	28	50	3	1074	104*	22.85	1	4	22
1913	23	43	3	1431	146*	35.77	3	7	19
1914	23	41	4	1265	227*	34.18	3	6	19
1919	16	30	2	699	82	24.96	-	5	11
1920	23	42	1	780	72	19.02	-	5	17
1921	27	51	2	1469	127	29.97	3	6	14
1922	26	47	2	1207	132	26.82	2	4	9
1923	22	39	3	1134	205	31.50	1	6	11
1924	24	41	3	831	92	21.86	-	5	16
1925	19	34	0	773	114	22.73	1	3	6
Total	**552**	**988**	**69**	**25122**	**227***	**27.33**	**34**	**130**	**339**

Notes: King played all his first-class cricket in England and Wales. He was dismissed 457 times caught (49%); 329 times bowled (36%); 67 times lbw (7%); 39 times stumped (4%); 23 times run out (3%); three times hit wicket, and once, famously, hit the ball twice. He retired hurt four times. The bowlers who took his wicket most often were W.Rhodes 23, G.H.Hirst 20, W.Bestwick 14, T.G.Wass 14, W.C.Smith 13, A.Warren 13, C.Blythe 12.

First-Class cricket: Batting and Fielding

	M	I	NO	R	HS	Ave	100	50	Ct
Leicestershire	502	896	64	22618	227*	27.18	32	115	308
MCC	36	67	1	1382	92	20.93	-	6	26
Players	5	9	3	468	109*	78.00	2	2	2
England XIs	4	7	0	294	72	42.00	-	3	1
England	1	2	0	64	60	32.00	-	1	-
North of England	1	1	0	92	92	92.00	-	1	1
J.Bamford's XI	1	2	0	71	60*	71.00	-	1	1
A.J.Webbe's XI	1	2	0	29	16	14.50	-	-	-
G.J.V.Weigall's XI	1	2	0	104	60	52.00	-	1	-
Total	**552**	**988**	**69**	**25122**	**227***	**27.33**	**34**	**130**	**339**

First-class cricket: Centuries (34)

Score	For	Opponent	Venue	Season
121	Leicestershire[1]	Derbyshire	Derby	1900
131	Leicestershire[1]	Hampshire	Southampton	1901
143	Leicestershire[1]	Derbyshire	Glossop	1901
135	Leicestershire[1]	London County	Leicester	1901
113*	Leicestershire[1]	Surrey	The Oval	1901
130	Leicestershire[2]	Worcestershire	Worcester	1902
109*	Leicestershire[2]	Worcestershire	Leicester	1902
127	Leicestershire[2]	Nottinghamshire	Trent Bridge	1903
167	Leicestershire[2]	Derbyshire	Leicester	1903
128	Leicestershire[1]	MCC	Lord's	1904
117*	Leicestershire[2]	Worcestershire	Leicester	1904
104	Players[1]	Gentlemen	Lord's	1904
109*	Players[2]	Gentlemen	Lord's	1904
186	Leicestershire[1]	Hampshire	Southampton	1904
126*	Leicestershire[1]	Derbyshire	Glossop	1906
118	Leicestershire[2]	Warwickshire	Leicester	1906
142	Leicestershire[1]	Northamptonshire	Northampton	1908
100*	Leicestershire[2]	Sussex	Leicester	1911
118	Leicestershire[1]	Hampshire	Leicester	1911
103*	Leicestershire[2]	Lancashire	Old Trafford	1911
104*	Leicestershire[1]	Worcestershire	Leicester	1912
111	Leicestershire[1]	Northamptonshire	Leicester	1913
100*	Leicestershire[2]	Northamptonshire	Leicester	1913
146*	Leicestershire[2]	Worcestershire	Worcester	1913
114*	Leicestershire[1]	Yorkshire	Leicester	1914
227*	Leicestershire[1]	Worcestershire	Coalville	1914
124	Leicestershire[1]	Northamptonshire	Northampton	1914
127	Leicestershire[2]	Surrey	Leicester	1921
110*	Leicestershire[2]	Sussex	Leicester	1921
125*	Leicestershire[1]	Lancashire	Old Trafford	1921
103	Leicestershire[1]	Kent	Leicester	1922
132	Leicestershire[1]	Hampshire	Southampton	1922
205	Leicestershire[1]	Hampshire	Leicester	1923
114	Leicestershire[1]	Sussex	Hove	1925

Notes: All the centuries scored by King at Leicester were at Aylestone Road. His Coalville century was at the Fox and Goose Ground.

Some Statistics

First-Class cricket: Bowling

	O	M	R	W	BB	Ave	5i	10m
1895	18	3	62	0	-	-	-	-
1897	85	17	229	2	1-18	114.50	-	-
1898	128.4	38	277	10	3-43	27.70	-	-
1899	438.4	145	967	22	4-12	43.95	-	-
1900	738	230	1793	81	7-91	22.13	7	1
1901	833.2	240	2081	80	7-51	26.01	5	2
1902	618.5	151	1732	68	6-32	25.47	5	-
1903	652.1	164	1681	63	5-6	26.68	2	-
1904	897	225	2277	78	7-32	29.19	4	2
1905	358.5	90	1070	40	5-39	26.75	3	-
1906	424.1	95	1192	38	4-23	31.36	-	-
1907	305	63	776	44	4-33	17.63	-	-
1908	679.1	144	1800	74	7-77	24.32	5	1
1909	660.1	155	1598	63	5-56	25.36	2	-
1910	6	0	27	1	1-27	27.00	-	-
1911	830.3	179	2294	73	8-17	31.42	4	1
1912	929.4	228	2293	130	8-26	17.63	16	2
1913	345	66	1002	27	4-104	37.11	-	-
1914	591.3	129	1452	70	5-26	20.74	3	-
1919	415.3	97	1028	37	6-36	27.78	2	-
1920	740.5	175	1765	100	8-61	17.65	8	2
1921	568	110	1540	55	5-86	28.00	1	-
1922	227.4	51	569	22	5-72	25.86	1	-
1923	236.4	68	596	23	5-31	25.91	1	-
1924	46	10	161	3	2-58	53.66	-	-
1925	20	2	50	0	-	-	-	-
Total 5b	670.3	202 ⎱							
6b	11104	2677 ⎰	30312	1204	8-17	25.17	69	11

Notes: From 1895 to 1899 there were 5 balls in an over, from 1900 to 1925 six balls in an over. King took wickets at the rate of one per 58.12 balls and conceded runs at a rate equivalent to 2.59 runs per six-ball over. Of his 1,204 wickets, 653 (54%) were caught; 363 (30%) bowled; 109 (9%) lbw; 69 (6%) were stumped and ten hit wicket. Of his 653 dismissals by catches, 87 were taken by identified wicket-keepers and 83 caught and bowled. The batsmen whom he dismissed most frequently were J.R.Gunn 16 times, C.Charlesworth 15, A.O.Jones 11, J.T.Tyldesley 11, S.W.A.Cadman 10, J.B.Hobbs 10, W.G.Quaife 10.

First-Class cricket: Bowling

	B	M	R	W	BB	Ave	5i	10m
Leicestershire	64579	2679	27780	1100	8-17	25.25	64	10
MCC	3970	145	1831	82	7-77	22.32	5	1
Players	144	4	68	3	2-37	22.66	-	-
England	162	5	99	1	1-99	99.00	-	-
England XIs	348	11	194	7	3-72	27.71	-	-
North of England	48	0	33	1	1-33	33.00	-	-
J.Bamford's XI	108	4	49	1	1-41	49.00	-	-
A.J.Webbe's XI	204	13	53	4	4-39	13.25	-	-
G.J.V.Weigall's XI	414	18	205	5	3-95	41.00	-	-
Total	69977	2879	30312	1204	8-17	25.17	69	11

Some Statistics

First-Class cricket: Five wickets or more in an innings (69)

Bowling	For	Opponent	Venue	Season
5-46	Leicestershire†	Nottinghamshire[1]	Leicester	1900
7-91	Leicestershire†	Yorkshire[1]	Huddersfield	1900
6-41	Leicestershire†	Worcestershire[1]	Leicester	1900
5-28	Leicestershire†	Worcestershire[2]	Leicester	1900
6-34	Leicestershire†	Worcestershire[1]	Worcester	1900
5-83	Leicestershire†	Essex[1]	Leicester	1900
5-36	Leicestershire†	Hampshire[2]	Southampton	1900
7-70	Leicestershire	Nottinghamshire[1]	Trent Bridge	1901
5-112	Leicestershire	Yorkshire[1]	Scarborough	1901
6-22	Leicestershire	Nottinghamshire[1]	Leicester	1901
7-51	Leicestershire†	Nottinghamshire[2]	Leicester	1901
5-65	Leicestershire†	Derbyshire[1]	Leicester	1901
5-72	Leicestershire†	Australians[1]	Leicester	1902
6-71	Leicestershire†	Sussex[1]	Leicester	1902
6-32	Leicestershire†	Warwickshire[1]	Leicester	1902
5-42	Leicestershire†	Nottinghamshire[1]	Leicester	1902
5-85	Leicestershire	Essex[2]	Leyton	1902
5-6	MCC	Sussex[1]	Lord's	1903
5-57	Leicestershire†	Sussex[1]	Hove	1903
7-55	Leicestershire	Warwickshire[1]	Edgbaston	1904
5-64	Leicestershire	Warwickshire[2]	Edgbaston	1904
7-32	Leicestershire†	London County[2]	Leicester	1904
5-55	Leicestershire†	Essex[2]	Leyton	1904
5-39	Leicestershire	Derbyshire[2]	Chesterfield	1905
5-46	Leicestershire†	Derbyshire[1]	Leicester	1905
5-58	Leicestershire	Lancashire[1]	Old Trafford	1905
5-51	Leicestershire	Warwickshire[2]	Leicester	1908
7-77	MCC	Cambridge Univ[1]	Lord's	1908
5-133	MCC	Cambridge Univ[2]	Lord's	1908
6-99	Leicestershire	Kent[1]	Canterbury	1908
5-52	Leicestershire	Surrey[1]	The Oval	1908
5-56	Leicestershire	Kent[1]	Leicester	1909
5-59	Leicestershire†	Nottinghamshire[1]	Leicester	1909
5-51	Leicestershire†	Lancashire[1]	Leicester	1911
5-50	Leicestershire†	Kent[1]	Leicester	1911
5-46	Leicestershire†	Worcestershire[1]	Leicester	1911
8-17	Leicestershire†	Yorkshire[2]	Leicester	1911
5-46	MCC	Yorkshire[1]	Lord's	1912
5-114	Leicestershire†	Lancashire[1]	Old Trafford	1912
5-132	Leicestershire†	Nottinghamshire[1]	Leicester	1912
8-26	Leicestershire†	Kent[1]	Leicester	1912
6-45	Leicestershire†	Worcestershire[1]	Stourbridge	1912
5-47	Leicestershire†	Warwickshire[1]	Nuneaton CC	1912
6-65	Leicestershire†	Derbyshire[1]	Ashby-de-la-Zouch 1912	
5-167	MCC†	Oxford University[1]	Lord's	1912
5-51	Leicestershire†	Surrey[1]	The Oval	1912
5-114	Leicestershire†	Hampshire[1]	Southampton	1912
5-53	Leicestershire†	Northamptonshire[1]	Leicester	1912
5-52	Leicestershire†	South Africans[1]	Leicester	1912
7-45	Leicestershire†	South Africans[2]	Leicester	1912
7-65	Leicestershire†	Kent[1]	Dover	1912
7-56	Leicestershire†	Warwickshire[1]	Hinckley (Ashby Rd) 1912	
5-87	Leicestershire†	Lancashire[1]	Leicester	1912
5-26	Leicestershire	Essex[2]	Leicester	1914
5-49	Leicestershire	Warwickshire[1]	Edgbaston	1914
5-53	Leicestershire†	Yorkshire[1]	Bradford	1914
5-45	Leicestershire	Northamptonshire[1]	Northampton	1919

137

Some Statistics

6-36	Leicestershire†	Gloucestershire[1]	Leicester	1919
7-46	Leicestershire†	Lancashire[1]	Old Trafford	1920
5-120	Leicestershire†	Kent[2]	Leicester	1920
8-61	Leicestershire†	Derbyshire[1]	Leicester	1920
5-41	Leicestershire†	Derbyshire[2]	Leicester	1920
5-81	Leicestershire	Surrey[1]	The Oval	1920
5-35	Leicestershire†	Northamptonshire[2]	Northampton	1920
6-63	Leicestershire	Gloucestershire[1]	Leicester	1920
7-34	Leicestershire	Somerset[2]	Weston-super-Mare	1920
5-86	Leicestershire	Glamorgan[2]	Swansea	1921
5-72	Leicestershire	Nottinghamshire[1]	Trent Bridge	1922
5-31	Leicestershire	Glamorgan[2]	Leicester	1923

Notes: The five-wicket returns obtained by King at Leicester in 1900 were at Grace Road; thereafter they were at Aylestone Road. Instances where King opened the bowling are shown by a dagger: there may be errors in the second innings for not all the scorebooks and scorecards have been seen or are in existence. The returns listed above include both his hat-tricks in first-class cricket: these were against Sussex at Hove in 1903 and against Somerset at Weston-super-Mare in 1920.

First-Class cricket: Ten wickets or more in a match (11)

Bowling	For	Opponent	Venue	Season
11-69 (6-41 and 5-28)	Leicestershire	Worcestershire	Leicester	1900
11-141 (7-70 and 4-71)	Leicestershire	Nottinghamshire	Trent Bridge	1901
13-73 (6-22 and 7-51)	Leicestershire	Nottinghamshire	Leicester	1901
12-119 (7-55 and 5-64)	Leicestershire	Warwickshire	Edgbaston	1904
10-58 (3-36 and 7-32)	Leicestershire	London County	Leicester	1904
12-210 (7-77 and 5-133)	MCC	Cambridge Univ	Lord's	1908
10-59 (2-42 and 8-17)	Leicestershire	Yorkshire	Leicester	1911
10-117 (6-65 and 4-52)	Leicestershire	Derbyshire	Ashby-de-la-Zouch	1912
12-97 (5-52 and 7-45)	Leicestershire	South Africans	Leicester	1912
11-98 (7-46 and 4-52)	Leicestershire	Lancashire	Old Trafford	1920
13-102 (8-61 and 5-41)	Leicestershire	Derbyshire	Leicester	1920

Note: The ten-wicket return obtained by King at Leicester in 1900 was at Grace Road; thereafter they were at Aylestone Road.

Teams

He played 502 first-class matches for Leicestershire, 36 for MCC and fourteen for other sides, including one Test match for England. He played 55 matches v Yorkshire, 46 v Warwickshire, 45 v Derbyshire, 45 v Nottinghamshire, 43 v Lancashire and 40 v Hampshire. In Championship cricket he scored most runs v Hampshire (2,255 at 37.58) and Derbyshire (2,223 at 32.21). His best batting averages were 51.22 v Worcestershire (for 1,844 runs) and 45.00 v Glamorgan (for 585 runs). He took most wickets v Nottinghamshire (111 at 24.09) and Derbyshire (105 at 23.37). His best bowling averages were 14.72 v Somerset (for 18 wickets), 14.78 v South Africans (for 23 wickets), 17.20 v Glamorgan (for 25 wickets), 17.96 v Gloucestershire (for 28 wickets) and 19.40 v Northamptonshire (for 60 wickets).

Grounds

During his first-class career he played on 57 different grounds, of which eight were in Yorkshire and six in Leicestershire. His most productive were Aylestone Road (9,729 runs at 28.36, 491 wickets at 22.43), Lord's (2,059 runs at 25.10, 111 wickets at 23.04), The Oval (1,088 runs at 30.22, 47 wickets at 25.74) and Southampton (1,085 runs at 54.25). At Grace Road his figures were 682 runs at 16.23 and 47 wickets at 33.02.

Sources: *Wisden's Cricketers' Almanack* and cricketarchive.com

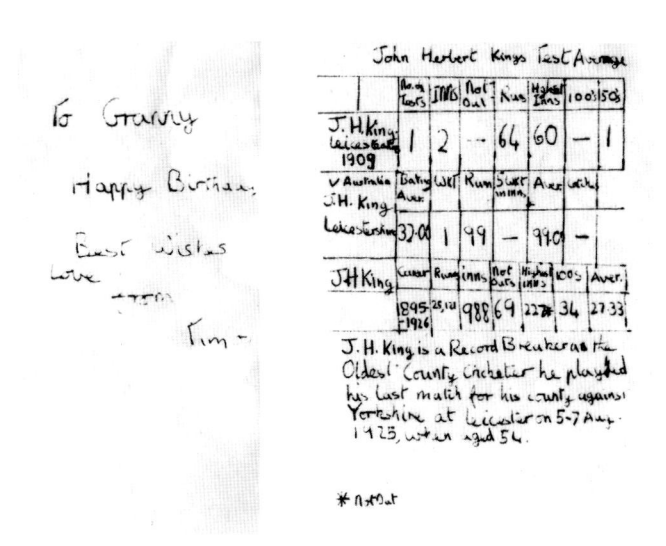

Timothy Cockroft, as a youngster, sent this record of his great-grandfather's first-class cricket as part of a birthday card to King's daughter, Margaret.

Appendix Two
King's Only Test Match

ENGLAND v AUSTRALIA
Played at Lord's Cricket Ground, St John's Wood, June 14, 15, 16, 1909.
Australia won by nine wickets.

ENGLAND

1	T.W.Hayward	st Carter b Laver	16	run out	6
2	J.B.Hobbs	c Carter b Laver	19	c and b Armstrong	9
3	J.T.Tyldesley	lbw b Laver	46	st Carter b Armstrong	3
4	G.Gunn	lbw b Cotter	1	b Armstrong	0
5	J.H.King	c Macartney b Cotter	60	b Armstrong	4
6	*A.C.MacLaren	c Armstrong b Noble	7	(8) b Noble	24
7	G.H.Hirst	b Cotter	31	b Armstrong	1
8	A.O.Jones	b Cotter	8	(6) lbw b Laver	26
9	A.E.Relf	c Armstrong b Noble	17	(10) b Armstrong	3
10	†A.F.A.Lilley	c Bardsley b Noble	47	(9) not out	25
11	S.Haigh	not out	1	run out	5
	Extras	b 8, lb 3, w 3, nb 2	16	b 2, lb 3, nb 10	15
			269		121

FoW (1): 1-23 (2), 2-41 (1), 3-44 (4), 4-123 (3), 5-149 (6), 6-175 (5), 7-199 (8), 8-205 (7), 9-258 (9), 10-269 (10)
FoW (2): 1-16 (2), 2-22 (3), 3-22 (4), 4-23 (1), 5-34 (5), 6-41 (7), 7-82 (8), 8-90 (6), 9-101 (10), 10-121 (11)

AUSTRALIA

1	P.A.McAlister	lbw b King	22	not out	19
2	F.J.Laver	b Hirst	14		
3	W.Bardsley	b Relf	46	(2) c Lilley b Relf	0
4	W.W.Armstrong	c Lilley b Relf	12		
5	V.S.Ransford	not out	143		
6	V.T.Trumper	c MacLaren b Relf	28		
7	*M.A.Noble	c Lilley b Relf	32		
8	S.E.Gregory	c Lilley b Relf	14	(3) not out	18
9	A.Cotter	run out	0		
10	C.G.Macartney	b Hirst	5		
11	†H.Carter	b Hirst	7		
	Extras	b 16, lb 8, w 1, nb 2	27	b 4	4
			350	(1 wicket)	41

FoW (1): 1-18 (2), 2-84 (1), 3-90 (3), 4-119 (4), 5-198 (6), 6-269 (7), 7-317 (8), 8-317 (9), 9-342 (10), 10-350 (11)
FoW (2): 1-4 (2)

King's Only Test Match

Australia Bowling

	O	M	R	W		O	M	R	W
Laver	32	9	75	3		13	4	24	1
Macartney	8	3	10	0					
Cotter	23	1	80	4	(2)	18	3	35	0
Noble	24.2	9	42	3	(3)	5	1	12	1
Armstrong	20	6	46	0	(4)	24.5	11	35	6

England Bowling

	O	M	R	W		O	M	R	W
Hirst	26.5	2	83	3		8	1	28	0
King	27	5	99	1					
Relf	45	14	85	5	(2)	7.4	4	9	1
Haigh	19	5	41	0					
Jones	2	0	15	0					

Umpires: C.E.Dench and J.Moss.   Toss: Australia
Close of Play: 1st day: Australia (1) 17-0 (McAlister 4*, Laver 13*); 2nd day: England (2) 16-1 (Hayward 5*).

Source: cricketarchive.com

Index

In the index below, a page number in parentheses indicates a periphrasis or the like (usually the name of a ground rather than of a county); a page number in bold type indicates an illustration. Of Appendix One only counties mentioned under 'Teams' (p 139) and players in notes (pp 134, 136) have been indexed.

Abel, R. 49
Achilles 44
Alderman Newton's School 7
All-England XI 22
Allsopp, T.C. **51**
Alma C.C. 60-61
architectural styles of batting 38
Armstrong, N.F. 96, 124
Armstrong, W.W. 50, 72, 74
Arnall-Thompson, H.T. 52, 124
Astill, W.E. 9, 28n, 39n, 46, 65, 68, 69, 72, 84, 85, 86, 95, 97, 99, 100, 101, 103, 104, 105, 106, 109, 110, 111, 112, 123, 124, 126-127, **87**, **98**
Australia/Australians 6, 18, 19, 26, 39n, 46, 50, 55, 63, 68, 69-75, 102-103, 140-141
Australian Imperial Services XI 96
Aylestone, Saint Andrew's Church 65, (115)

back play 31, 34-35
Baker, G.R. 25
Balderstone, J.C. 28n
Bale, F. 9
Bamford's XI 68
Bannerman, C. 18
Bardsley, W. 74
Barnes, S.F. 69, 94
bat, weight of 36
Beldam, G.W. 29, 30, 32, 34, 37, 39, 59, 70
Belton, T. 80n
Belvedere College, Dublin 44
Benskin, W.E. 101, 106, **98**

Berry, G.L. (L.G.) 114, 124
Bestwick, W. 52, 134n
billiards 112
Birkenhead Park C.C. 21-25, 27, 30, 46, 71, 108, 126
Birkenshaw, J. 28n
Bisset, A.V.C. 60, **61**
Bisset, Sir Murray 60, **61**
Bland, C.H.G. 52
Blücher, G.B. von 81
Blythe, C. 39, 42, 69, 70, 71, 84, 85, 88, 134n
Boone, Willie 117
Bosanquet, B.J.T. 55, 74
Bottrill, F.W. (printer and employer) 15
bowled, thirteen batsmen in a row 97
Bradford Cricket League 93-94
Bradman, Sir Donald 6, 127n
Braund, L.C. 56
Brearley, W. 70, 72
Briers, N.E. 14
Brown, Arthur (friend) 66-67
Brown, J.T. 42
Brown, W. **87**
Brus, Robert de 14
Buchanan, R. **61**
Bunyan, John 47
Burdett, T. **51**
Burns, Robert 63
Burrows, R.D. 84n
Butt, H.R. 52
Byron, Lord 63

Cadman, S.W.A. 136n

143

Index

Callington, A. s.v. Lord, A.
Cambridge University C.C. 14, 16, 26, 47, 49, 54, 59n, 68, 99
  Christ's College 7, 8, 114
  Hawks' Club 8
Cambridgeshire C.C.C. 110, 123
Cape Town C.C. 60
Cardus, Sir Neville 127n
Carlin, J. 49
Carolin, H.W. 61, **61**
Cassandra 70
Charles I 13
Charles II 13
Charlesworth, C. 136n
Cheshire C.C.C. 21, 22n
Claremont C.C. 60
Clarke, Ernest (county supporter) 88
Clay, J.C. 106
Clift, P.B. 28n
Coalville, Fox & Goose Ground 88
Cockroft, Georgina (great granddaughter) 117
Cockroft, Judy (granddaughter) 6, 112, 116, 118
Cockroft, Richard (grandson-in-law) 116, (118)
Cockroft, Timothy (great-grandson) 116-117, 139, **117**
Coe, S. 28n, 36, 53, 54, 67, 74, 80, 89, 95, 108, 121, 127, **25, 51, 98**
Colbeck, L.G. 59n
Cole, Ann s.v. King, Ann
Cole, Barbra (ancestor) 13
Cole, Richard (ancestor) 14
Cole, Colonel William (ancestor) 13
Collins, H.L. 96
Commonwealth, The 13
Cook, N.G.B. 14
Cook, S.J. 81
Cotter, A. 72
Coustouce, Mr (farmer and employer) 91
Cowdrey, M.C. 38n
Cox, G.R. 52
Crawford, J.N. 39, 59, 94
Crawford, V.F.S. 46, 127, **51**
Creber, H. 103

Curtis, J.S. 85, 97

Dakin, J.M. 28n
Darling, J. 50
Davis, A.E. **51**
Davis, R.B. 106
Davison, B.F. 124
DeFreitas, P.A.J. 28n
Dempster, C.S. 100
Denton, D. 26, 94, 113
Derbyshire C.C.C. 18, 25, 37, (46), 47, 49, 52, 54, 62, (64), 65, 67n, 85, (86), 97, 98, 99, 103, 106, 109n, 114, 124, 139
de Trafford, C.E. 31, 38, 95, 108n, 127, **25, 98**
Devon Dumplings C.C. 116
Devonshire, Duke and Duchess of 114
Dexter, E.R. 38n
Difford, A.N. **61**
Diocesan College 60
d'Oliveira, B.L. 69
Douglas, J.W.H.T. 59, 88
Doyle, Sir Arthur Conan 51
drives 31-34
Duckworth, L.H. 94
Duleepsinhji, K.S. 56
Durham C.C.C. 103, 110, 123

Eccleshill C.C. 93
Edmund Ironside 80
Edward II 80
Elmhirst, Rev E. 16, 31, **17**
Elston, C. 21
Emmett, T. 26, 31, 34, 43, **51**
England XIs 50, 58, 68, 71, 87
Essex C.C.C. 19-20, 47, 64, 87, 103, (108)
Eton v Harrow 114
Evans, E.G. 30

Faulkner, G.A. 85
Felix, N. 30
Field, E.F. (F.E.) 67
Fielder, A. 88
Fingleton, J.H.W. 127n
forward play 30-32

Foster, R.E. 56
Fowke, G.H.S. 100, 110
Freeman, A.P.F. 39n, 104
Freemasons 13, 112, 113
  Wiclif Lodge 13, 112
  Syston Lodge 112
Fry, C.B. 29, 31, 32, 34, 35, 37, 39-40, 42, 68, 69, 119, 125

Gaunt, John of 13
Geary, G. 9, 28n, 39, 80, 84, 86, 87, 90, 95, 97, 104, 105, 106, 108, 109, 110, 124, **87**
Geeson, F. 20, 45, 47, 49, 50, **25**
Gentlemen of England 16, 54
Gentlemen v Players 16, 55-59, 60, 71, 86, 114, 124-125, 127
Gill, G.C. 51, **51**
Gillespie-Stainton, R.W. 16
Gillette Cup competition 67n
Gilligan, A.E.R. 108, 113n
Gladstone, W.E. 19
Glamorgan C.C.C. 103, 105, 106, 109, 139
Gloucestershire C.C.C. 50n, 97, 103, 105, 108, 139
Gooch, G.A. 36
googly 74, 83-84
Gordon, Sir Home 72
Gower, D.I. 38n
Grace, E.M. 35
Grace, W.G. 47, 49, 50-51, 59, 62, 83, 97, 109n, 121-122
Granby, Marquis of 48
Great Horton C.C. 93
Green Point C.C. 60
Gregory, J.M. 6, 8, 96, 102
Grey, Lady Jane 13
Gunn, G. 69, 72, 94
Gunn, J.R. 28-29, 32, 37, 38n, 40, 42n, 44, 136n

Haddon Hall 66
Haigh, G. 74
Haigh, S. 39, 69, 72, 94
Halford, Sir Richard (ancestor) 13
Hallam, A.W. 39
Hallam, M.R. 38n, 124

Hallows, C. 99, 103
Hallows, J. 39
Hambledon C.C. 68, 101
Hampshire C.C.C. 38, 47, 49, 52, 53, 65, 83, (86), 98, 99, (104), 105, 124, 139
Hanif Mohammad 28n
Hardstaff, J. (sen) 59
Harmison, S.J. 7
Harold II Godwinson 80
Harrison, G.C. 99
Harrow School 16
Harry, Prince 14
Harte F.B. (Bret) 121
Hathorn, C.M.H. 58
Haverford College 60
Hawke, Lord 21, 24, 26, 69, 74, 100, 113
Hayward, T.W. 55, 64, 69, 72, 74
Hazlerigg, Sir Arthur 64, 76, 77
Hazlerigg family 11n
Headley, G.A. 48n
Hearne, A. 39
Hearne, J.T. 56
Hearne, J.W. 94
Henderson, C.W. 28n
Hesketh-Prichard, H.V. 55, 56
Hicks, W.A. **61**
Higgins, G.F. 20
Highgate School 44
Hill, A.J.L. 49
Hillyard, G.W. 21
Hinckley Grammar School 15
Hirst, G.H. 20, 23, 28n, 39n, 46, 70, 71, 73, 74, 80, 81, 85, 86, 87, 88, 126, 134n
Hitch, J.W. 94, 103
hitting the ball twice 64, 125
Hobbs, J.B. 38, 59, 68, 72, 86, 94, 106n, 125, 126n, 136n
Hoi Pepnumenoi C.C. 23
Holden, C. 22, 23, 24
Horace (Roman poet) 30
Hubbard, J.H. 15
Hue-Williams, Mark 117
Hurlingham C.C. 117
Hutchinson, J.M. 106

145

Index

Idle C.C. 93
Illingworth, R. 28n
Irving, G. 15
Isaacs, Sir Rufus 69
I Zingari 16

Jackson, Hon F.S. 26, 69
Jackson, V.E. 28n, 83
James II 13
Jardine, D.R. 114n
Jayes, T. 59, 69, 70, 71, 72, 121
Jephson, D.L.A. 34, 49
Jessop, G.L. 26, 56, 59, 69, 70
Jones, A.O. 136n
Jones, P.S.T. **61**
Julian, R. 127
Jupp, V.W.C. 95

Kasprowicz, M.S. 28n
Keighley C.C. 94
Kennedy, A.S. 105
Kent C.C.C. 68, 84, 85, (88), 103, 104, (105), 106, (108), (109), 124, 125
Kilburn, J.M. 119
Kilner, R. 105
King, Ann (née Cole, mother) 13, 14, 15, 90
King, Annie Matilda (sister) 14
King, Carol Angela Florence (granddaughter) **115**
King, Charles (half-brother) 13
King, Emma (sister) 14
King, Florence (née Norton, wife) 66-67, 92, 93, 115, **66**
King, James (brother) 7, 11, 14, 19, 45, 46, 63, 116, 118, **51**
  letter of 11, **11**
  gravestone of **128**
King, James Temple (father) 12, 13, 14, 17, 21, 27, 53, 71n, 93, **12**
King, J.B. 53
King, Colonel John (ancestor) 11

King, John Herbert
  ancestry 11-14
  for J.Bamford's XI 68

bat 36, **58**
batting technique and style 29-38, 120-121, **29**, **30**, **33**
benefit matches 78, 106, **79**, **107**
best innings analysis (progressive) 26, 46, 47, 49, 81-83
best match analysis 49
best second-innings analysis 54
and Birkenhead Park C.C. 21-27, 30, 46, 71, 108, 126
bowling technique 38-44, **41**
bowling unchanged 46, 47, 61, 85, 97
business interests 15, 45, 92-93
captain v Lancashire 110
cartoon **75**
century in Bradford League 93
at Christ's College, Cambridge 8, 114
coaching 22, 60, 86, 113, 114
cricketing longevity 95-96, 106, 108-109, 125
with daughter **66**
death 116
début for Leicestershire 18, 19-20
the 'double' 84, 101, 124
double-centuries 88-89, 105-106
and Eccleshill C.C. 93
education 14, 15
in England cap **4**
for England XIs 50, 58, 68, 87
for England v Australia 69-75, 140-141
field placing 43
first wicket 25
first five-wicket innings 46-47
first ten-wicket match 46
first half-century 24
first century 47
first century by a professional for Birkenhead Park 24
first century of the season 108
fielding 44, 121
first catch 20
first Leicestershire player to appear in a home Test 71, 124
and gardening 66, 78, 92, 93, 112

146

Index

going out to bat **back cover**
and googlies 74, 83-84
with granddaughter Carol **115**
gravestone 118, **128**
grounds played on 139
on Ground Staff at Lord's 22, 45, 55
in group photographs **25, 51, 61, 87, 98**
'hat-tricks' and near-misses 47, 49, 52, 99, 124, 125
health 44, 45, 78, 96, 101, 105, 113
highest score (progressive) 19, 24, 26, 47, 49, 52, 53, 88-89
hit the ball twice 64, 125
homes 45, 53, 67, 92, 115, 116, **92**
injuries 6, 50, 62, 65, 76, 78, 80, 84n, 89, 102, 105, 108
and leisure pursuits 66, 92, 112
letter to S.C.Packer 76-78
and Liberal Club 112
for Liverpool and District 26
and 'lobsters' 49, (50)
long spells 24-25, 50, 68, 85, 86, 104
loyalty to Leicestershire 101, 126
and Lutterworth Cricket Club 15, 16-17, 31
marriage 65-66, **65**
and masons 112, 113
for M.C.C. 45n, 46, 47, 49, 50, 51, 52-53, 54, 63, 65, 68, 84, 85, 93, 96, 110, 123, 139
most productive grounds 139
for North v South 54
opening batting 62, 97
opening batting and bowling 62
opening bowling 26, 39, 46, 61, 62, 65, 71-72, 85
physique 14, 30, 120
played v nineteen counties 110, 123
for Players v Gentlemen 55-59, 124-125, 127
presentation made to him and C.J.B.Wood **83**

record wicket partnerships 52, 54
retired hurt four times in career 126
outside 'Rutland House' **92**
at Scarborough Festival 54, 113
scorebooks showing his achievements **52, 57, 82, 90, 99, 109**
senior professional 100-101
siblings 13, 14 (see also King, James)
for Single v Married 26
'spectacles' 20, 46, 85
street named after him 116
talent-money 48, 54, 68, 80, 111
Chevallier Tayler's drawing **30**
telegram sent to him **73**
temperament 32, 36-37, 100-101, 121, 122
on tour of northern Scotland 105
two centuries in a match 56-58, 86, 103, 124-125, 127
umpiring 8, 23, 45n, 113-114, 115
upbraided by Lord Hawke 100
waistcoat button **101**
'walking' 94
war-time employment 91, 92
for A.J.Webbe's XI 49
for G.J.V.Weigall's XI 54
and Western Province C.C. 60-62, **61**
with wife and daughter **66**
youthful non-cricketing sporting interests 14, 15

King, John William (nephew) 7, 116
King, Margaret Bruce (daughter) s.v. Wearn, Margaret Bruce
King, Matilda (great-great grandmother ?) 11
King, William (half-brother) 13
Knight, A.E. 9, 19, 20-21, 23, 25, 26, 31, 34-35, 36-37, 43, 44, 50, 51, 52, 53, 54, 56, 59, 64, 68, 71n, 72n, 80, 89, 116, 119-122, 124, **25, 29, 51, 65, 119**

147

Index

Knight, B.R. 28n
Kortright, C.J. 20, 43, 125-126
Kotze, J.J. 54, 58, 60, 61, **61**

Lambert, W. 16
Lancashire C.C.C. (25), 62, 68, 71n, 80, 81, 83, 84, 85, 86, 88, (98), 103, 104, (110), 124, 125, 126, 139
Langridge, James 28
Larwood, H. 6
Laughton, Manor at 13
Laver, F.J. 72, 73
Lawrence, A.J. (printer and employer) 45
left-handedness 28, 34n
left-handed all-rounders 28
leg-side strokes 35-36
Leicester
  Aylestone Road Ground 6, 7, 8, 47-48, (67), 91-92, 96, 105, (121), **48, 51, 91, 102**
  Grace Road Ground 8, 10, 17, 18-19, 47, 63, (66), 67, (120), **19**
  Wharf Street Ground 18
Leicester v Coventry (1788) 64
Leicester Cricket Association 17
Leicester Ivanhoe C.C. 23
Leicester Liberal Club Billiards Cup 112, **112**
Leicester Literary and Philosophical Society 119n
Leicester Town Club 63
Leicestershire C.C.C.
  1897 **25**
  1903 **51**
  1913 **87**
  1920 **98**
Leicestershire Volunteer Regiment 92
Lester, G. 28n
Lester, J.A. 60
Leveson-Gower, Sir Henry 69, 70
Lewis, C.C. 28n
Leyland C.C. 24
Lilley, A.F.A. 74
Lincoln, Bishop of 14
Lingard (umpire at Eccleshill) 93

Liverpool and District 21n, 26
Lock, G.A.R. 28n, 123
London County C.C. 49, 50, 51, 54, 60, 110, 123
longevity of cricketers 95-96, 106, 108, 109n
Lord, A. 80, **87**
Lord's, ground staff at 22, 45, 55
Loughborough Grammar School 15
Ludgrove Preparatory School 14
Lutterworth
  Congregational Chapel 14, (15)
  Cricket Club (15), 16-17, 31
  Grammar School 14, 15
  Manor of 13
  St Mary's Church 12, 14, 116, 118, **12**

McAlister, P.A. 73
Macartney, C.G. 72-73
Macaulay, G.G. 105, 110
McDonald, E.A. 6, 8, 102
McDonell, H.C. 99
MacLaren, A.C. 62, 69, 70, 74, 106n
McVicker, N.M. 28n
Maddy, D.L. 28n
Manchester C.C. 23
Mancroft, Lord 47
Manners, John 65
Marlborough College 14
Marner, P.T. 28n
Marriott, C. 16, 17, **17**
Marriott, H.H. 14
Mary, Queen 13
Masons s.v. Freemasons
May, P.B.H. 38n
MCC 7, 16, 17, 20, 22., 45n, 46, 47, 49, 50, 52, 54, 55, 63, 64, 65, 68, 71n, 84, 85, 93, 96, 110, 114, 123, 139
MCC tourists to Australia 68
Mead, C.P. 99, 100
Mead, W. 39
medical treatment at Leicester 78
Michael, Sylvia 8
Middlesex C.C.C. 26, 27, 46, 50, 59n, 97, 103

148

Index

Midlands Knock-out Competition 67n
Millns, D.J. 28n
Millward, A. 64
Minor Counties, 45n, 49
Moore, F.B. **61**
Moore, Frankfort 114
Morton, A. 114
Mounteney, A. 101, 102, **87, 98**
Munden, V.S. 28n, 83
Mynn, A. 18

Nayudu, C.K. 106n
Nestor 100
New Brighton C.C. 23, 24
Newman, J.A. 99, 105
Nichols, J. 13
Noble, M.A. 50, 72, 74
North America 26
North v South 16, 18, 54
Northamptonshire C.C.C. 62, 67, 68, 71n, 86, 88, 89, 97, 98, 103, 104, 124, 139
Norton, Elizabeth (sister-in-law) 92
Norton, Florence s.v. King, Florence
Nottinghamshire C.C.C. 19, (44), 47, 49-50, (52), 63, 78, 85, (97), (104), 108, 122, 124, 139
Nourse, A.W. ('Dave') 85, 106n.

Odell, W.W. 50, 59, 95, **51**
Old Gooseberry Show Society 14
Oldfield, N. 71n
Ormskirk C.C. 25
Osborn, F. **87**
Oxford University C.C. 16, 60, 85, 110, 113, 114
Oxford v Cambridge matches 16, 114

Packer, S.C. 76-78, **78, 87, 98**
Pakistan 7, 28n
Palmer, C.H. 28n, 83, 125
Parkin, C.H. 94
Parsons, G.J. 28n
Philadelphians 53
Pickett, H. 19-20
Players of the South 54

Pochin, Victor (friend) 114n
Pollock, R.G. 38
Potter, L. 28n
Pougher, A.D. 17, 20, 23, 28n, 45, 52, 71n, 84, 120, 124, **25**
Psellos, Michael 77
push stroke 31
Pycroft, J. 30

Quaife, W.G. 108, 109n, 136n

Rain, -. (Alma C.C.) 61
Ranjitsinhji, K.S. 34, 35, 36, 58, 125
Ransford, V.S. 73, 74
Read, W.W. 71n
Redgate, S. 18
Reeves, W. 96
Reid, A. 60, **61**
Relf, A.E. 44, 69
'Reynard' 17, 45, 68, 78
Rhodes, W. 20n, 28n, 39, 42, 46, 56, 69, 105, 126, 134n
Richardson, T. 49
Riley, W.N. 95, **87**
Robert I the Bruce, King of the Scots 14, 64, 80
Robertson, W.P. 74
Robertson-Glasgow, R.C. 96, 99 (caption)
Robinson, E. 105
Rock Ferry C.C. 23
Root, C.F. 18, 43, 46, 48, 96
Rose, W.G. (friend) 15
Rossall School 16
Routledge, T.W. 71
Rupert, Prince 47
Russell, C.A.G. (A.C.) 88
Rutland, Duke of 18
Rylott, A. 22, 43, 45, 120, **22**

Sadiq Mohammad 28n
Salmon, G.H. 9
Sargent, M.A.J. 93
Saturday starts in Championship 67
Saunders, P.F. 93
Sawrey-Cookson, Toby 117

149

Index

Scarborough Festival 54, 113
Schultz, S.S. 71n
Scotland, Leicestershire's tour in north of 105
Scott, Sir Gilbert 12
Seddon, Rev R. (headmaster) 15
Sefton Park C.C. 23, 63
Sellers, A.B. 114n
Sharp, A.T. 9, 88, 100, 101, 115
Sharp, J. 75
Sharp, J.A.T. (General Sir John) 115
Shaw, A. 42
Sheffield, crowd at Bramall Lane 121
Shields, J. 85, **87**
Shingler, G. **98**
Shipman, A.W. 9, 28n, 62, 101
Shipman, W. 85, 86, 101, **87**
shooting 66, 92, 112, 116
Shuttleworth, Rev B. 13
Shuttleworth, R. 13
Sidwell, T.E. 9, **98**
Simmons, P.V. 28n
Simpson-Hayward, G.H.T. 49, 50
Single *v* Married 26
Skelding, A. 86, 87, 94, 96, 114n, 127, **87, 98**
Smart, J. (friend) 15
Smart T.S. (friend) 15
Smith, E. 21, 22, 23, 27
Smith, Gunner **61**
Smith, H.A. 124
Smith, H.A.H. 84
Smith, W.C. 134n
Smith-Bingham, Guy 117
Snooke, S.D. 60
Snooke, S.J. 60
Snow, C.P. (Lord Snow) 6, 8, 9n
Snow, E.E. 6, 9n, 11, 19, 67n
Snow, H. 6
Snow, P.A. 6-9, 10, 39, 63, 114
Somerset C.C.C. 81, 99, 103, 124, 139
South Africa/South Africans 49, 54, 58, 60, 71, 85
South Africa College 60
Southwell, Bishop of 97
Spencer, C.T. 124

Spofforth, F.R. 19
Spooner, R.H. 62
Steele, J.F. 28n, 124
Stocks, F.W. 47, **25, 51**
Suffolk, Duke of (Henry Grey) 13
Surrey C.C.C. 26, 27, (46), (47), 48, (49), 63, (64), (65), (68), 83, 84, (88), (90), 103, 105, 121, 124, 125
Sussex C.C.C. 52-53, 58, 62, 83, 97, 103, 104, 105, (108), 109, 124
Sutcliffe, H. 94
Swaythling, Lord and Lady 114
Synge, A. 70

Taberer, H.M. 60, **61**
Talbot, A.B. 80
Tancred, L.J. 85
Tate, M.W. 96, 108
Tayler, Arnold Chevallier, drawing by 29, 32, **30**
Taylor, C.H. 105, 111
Taylor, H.W. 85
Taylor, S. **98**
  scorecard in hand of **89**
Tennyson, Hon L.H. 99
Tennyson, Alfred, Lord 16
Thompson, G.J. 69
Thomson, A.A. 56, 74
Titchmarsh, C.H. 110
Tomlin, W. 120, **25**
Tompkin, M. 7, 32
Tong Park C.C. 93
Town, E. 22
Townshend, Rev W. 16, **17**
Trott, A.E. 36
Trumble, H. 39
Trumper, V.T. 50, 74
Tuchman, B.W. 91
Tunnicliffe, J. 26
Turner, M.F. 9, 67n
two centuries in a match 16, 56-58, 86, 103, 124-125, 127
Tyldesley, G.E. (Ernest) 94, 99
Tyldesley, J.T. 55, 56, 72, 136n

Ullesthorpe 16
Uppingham Rovers 120

Uppingham School 12, 71n

van Geloven, J. 28n
Verdum, Roaesia de 13
Vernon, Dorothy 65

Wadlow, Captain **61**
'walking' 94
Walsh, J.E. 28n, 93, 123, 124, 127
Wanostrocht, N. s.v. Felix, N.
Ward, W. 36
Warner, Sir Pelham 36
Warren, A. 134n
Warwickshire C.C.C. (20), 24, 53, 54, 62, 64, 67, 68, 85, (88), 97, 105, 108, 109n, (110), 124
Wass, T.G. 122, 134n
Waterloo, battle of 81
Wearn, Christopher (grandson) 71n, 116
Wearn, Margaret Bruce (daughter) 6, 10, 15, 63, 66, 67, 77, 78, 80, 92, 96, 100, 101, 102n, 112, 113, 114, 115, 116, 126, **66, 115**
Webbe's XI 49
Weigall's XI 54
Wellington College 84
Wellington, Duke of 81
Wells, V.J. 28n
West, W.A.J. 64
Western Province C.C. 60-62, **61**
West Indies 71n
Wheeler, J.H. 45
Whitaker, J.J. 124
White, B. (friend) 108
Whitehead, H. 54, 86, 88, 89, 90, 122, 123, **51, 87, 98**

Whiteside, J.P. 43, 45, 120, **25**
Whittle, Sir Frank 116
William II 80
William III 13
William, Prince 14
Wilson, G.A. 50
Winchester School 16, 114n
Winterton, E.G. 7-8
Winterton, Rt Hon. Rosalie 7
Wood, C.J.B. 20, 25, 28n, 38, 46, 48, 49, 50, 51, 59, 81, 86, 93, 95, 97, 100, 123, 127, **25, 51, 83, 87, 98**
Wood, R. 71n
Woodcock, A. 20, 26, 43, 45, 46, 50, 60, 127, **25**
Woolley, F.E. 28, 88, 94, 104
Worcestershire C.C.C. 7, 18, 46, 47, 49, 50, 53, 64, 84, 85, 86, (87), 88-89, 90, 103, 116, 122, 124, 139
World War I 34, 89, 91-92, 94, 95, **91**
 memorial service for 97
Wyatt, R.E.S. 105
Wycliffe, John 13, 14
Wyggeston Grammar School (9), 15, 119

Yardley, N.W.D. 8
York, Mrs (landlady) 45
Yorkshire C.C.C. 8, 10, 20, 21, 26, 46, 47, 49, 50, 52, 62, 80, 81-83, 85, (86), (87), 88, 95, 96n, 97, 103, (105), 110, 121, 122, 124, 125, 139
Young, H.I. 47